GPH: *AN INFORMAL RECORD*

NUMBER 13
IN THE SERIES OF KEEPSAKES
ISSUED BY
THE FRIENDS OF THE BANCROFT LIBRARY
FOR ITS MEMBERS

AN INFORMAL RECORD

OF GEORGE P. HAMMOND AND HIS ERA

IN THE

BANCROFT LIBRARY

THE FRIENDS OF THE BANCROFT LIBRARY
UNIVERSITY OF CALIFORNIA
MCMLXV

Table of Contents

List of Illustrations

Foreword

On July 1, 1946, George Peter Hammond entered the doors of the Bancroft Library at the University of California and hung up his hat, prepared to stay a while—a stay that has extended through nineteen years. George is a man of ideas; and a man, moreover, disposed to implement his ideas with action. Just a month after he returned to his alma mater as Director of an institution in which he had once labored as a student assistant, George brought into being the Friends of the Bancroft Library. Thus our organization has a life-span almost exactly equal to the Hammond tenure in Berkeley.

The organizing meeting was held at the Bohemian Club in San Francisco. Henry R. Wagner, with his unique qualities as a catalyst, made one of his rare sallies up from San Marino for the occasion. He was then in his 84th year. The others present, besides the ubiquitous Hammond, were Carl I. Wheat, Charles L. Camp, George R. Stewart, George L. Harding, Warren R. Howell, and Francis P. Farquhar, distinguished scholars and bookmen all. That the Friends of these latter days may appreciate how accurately the charter members sized up the need, and how faithfully their objectives have been pursued over the years, let us print the agreement drawn up at that urbane luncheon meeting:

The undersigned hereby agree to form a non-profit organization entitled THE FRIENDS OF THE BANCROFT LIBRARY. *The headquarters and permanent address will be the Bancroft Library, University of California, Berkeley 4, California.*

The object of the Friends is to raise funds for the purpose of supplementing the ordinary funds of the Bancroft Library which are in the course of natural busi-ness appropriated for the purchase of books for the library by the institution.

The affairs of the Friends shall be conducted by a Board of Governors con-sisting of (originally 8, later 16) members, who shall have sole charge of the affairs of the Friends. The Board of Governors shall be self-perpetuating. When any member of the Board becomes incapacitated, or resigns, or dies, the remain-ing members shall choose from the general body of the members of the Friends a successor or successors.

1 August 1946
San Francisco, California

That is how it all began. Before two years passed, the Friends could muster 150 members, and showed every evidence of growing into a really useful organization. The first publication by the Friends, an *Annual Letter* mailed to the members over the signature of Chairman George L. Harding, was printed in September, 1948. Next year we got out our first book, the noble *Treaty of Guadalupe Hidalgo*, edited by our man GPH and printed by the Grabhorn Press; and early in

1950 that light-hearted link between the Friends and the Library, *Bancroftiana,* began to enliven the Bancroft scene.

I have no intention here, where all are at my mercy, of embarking upon a complete history of our organization. We are bringing you, with the wholehearted cooperation of George's long-time friends and associates, a many-sided account of GPH and his labors for the Bancroft Library, and the spotlight should rest upon George and the Library. Still, we claim descent from the fertile mind of this resourceful fellow, and some of the Friends' experiences as an organization George must account among the memorable moments of his long life.

Many of these high points have been associated with our Annual Meetings, held in the Library in the spring. The forthcoming meeting of May 23, 1965, when GPH will be surprised by formal presentation of this book, is the eighteenth in a series that began in 1948. Appropriately, the first speaker ever to address the Friends was Herbert E. Bolton, with some "Reminiscences of the Bancroft Library." Seven years later, we listened to Carl I. Wheat's challenging address commemorative of the fiftieth anniversary of this Library at the University of California, an address which recalled to us its great history, and bade us consider well its future. (How much we regret, Carl, the illness that has beset you, and of late prevented you from bringing to the Annual Meeting your wisdom, your humor, your energy, and your personal warmth. We all admire your long steadfastness and scholarly activity in the face of physical adversity, and have an abiding sense of your presence among us.)

At the Annual Meeting of 1961 we were enabled to tell the Friends of the acquisition of the papers and library of Don Silvestre Terrazas, a great collection centering upon the Mexican Revolution of 1910 and its aftermath. That purchase was a joint undertaking by the Friends and the University, like the recent acquisition of the Honeyman Collection as described herein by Susanna Dakin. Really major undertakings of this kind date from our efforts to acquire the Portolá Documents in 1957—papers of Gaspar de Portolá, first governor of California, surviving from that truly pioneer era, 1769–1770. We campaigned to raise the money for that purchase; we were successful; and we have gone on to progressively larger things.

A mighty help in the enlarged usefulness of the Friends was the major expansion of the membership in 1958–1959, when nearly 600 University of California alumni responded to appeals that they support the pride and special glory of their alma mater. Some of the Friends—too many—have passed on, but other staunch supporters of the Library have taken their place. Our membership, as this volume goes to press, totals approximately 1,000. We are not satisfied to remain at that level: consider how much more effective we could be if we numbered 10,000 members! But we have an excellent working base; we propose to go on working; and we have legally incorporated the Friends as a non-profit body, having permanence and accountability in the eyes of the law.

The occasion of George P. Hammond's retirement from the Bancroft Library has given us a fitting opportunity to honor him—and at the same time view the Library itself in fresh perspective. In the light of what is said in these pages, all will have a clearer idea where the Bancroft Library has come from, where it is going—and how we can help it get there. GPH, a modest man, may feel that this is the real importance of, and perhaps the only justification for, such a book as this. But we want him to know, in the way he likes best—through the publication of a book—that we are glad he came along when he did, a man of rare capacities to do the job that so badly needed doing. George's successor may find that he has greater freedom to achieve for the Library, relieved of the necessity to wrestle constantly and wearyingly with structural matters fundamental to everything else. We promise him our support, and he will hear similarly from GPH, let no one doubt.

George's friends and colleagues who have contributed to this Keepsake are men and women of such distinction that I positively decline to "introduce" them, but it affords me pleasure to observe that four of the original eight Friends are represented in these pages, including George himself (abducted into the book by main force). Charles Camp, I might note (for he does not), over many years was vitally concerned with Bancroft as a member of the Academic Senate's Bancroft Library Subcommittee of the Committee on the Library—a potent force on the campus. Two other contributors are prominent members of the Bancroft staff—Dale Morgan and Bob Becker, the latter now Assistant Director. Jim Holliday remains a Bancrofter in marvelously good standing—everybody cheers up when he comes around—though after two and a half years as Assistant Director he yielded to the charms of teaching, like Bob Burke before him, and currently instructs the young at San Francisco State College. The estimable Burke now holds forth in Seattle, as chairman of the history department at the University of Washington, a post almost as interesting as his old Bancroft job, which he describes for us. Susanna Dakin and Warren Howell, when not writing or ferreting out books (and pictures), are valiant members of the Friends' governing Council, and the same must be said of Francis Farquhar. If we see Agapito Rey and France Scholes less often, the overpowering attraction of GPH or the Bancroft Library nevertheless brings them in our direction every now and then, and we will always consider them part of the family.

Dale Morgan's account of GPH appeared originally, in shorter form, in *Pacific Historian*, August, 1963. France Scholes's address to the Academy of American Franciscan History on December 28, 1964, like GPH's response, is printed by courtesy of the Academy. For Jim Holliday's address to the California Historical Society on the occasion of the Wagner award, September 25, 1964, we are indebted to the Society as well as the author. We have helped ourselves to George's first publication, one of the most interesting features of this book. Otherwise, everything now printed has been especially written for us. To Messrs. Rey, Camp, Becker, Burke, Howell, and Farquhar, and to Mrs. Dakin, we express our appreciation for this whole-hearted cooperation, at the same time thanking our other authors—GPH included. It is altogether fitting that a book about GPH should be printed by Lawton Kennedy, in view of their long professional and personal association; he, too, is one of the creators of our informal tribute to George P. Hammond.

O. CORT MAJORS, *Chairman of the Council*

THE FRIENDS OF THE BANCROFT LIBRARY

GPH

DALE L. MORGAN

George P. Hammond, "GPH," is familiar to the broad community of scholarship as the most eminent living student of the Spanish Southwest, author and editor of an imposing number of books and monographs relating to the early history of Mexico, New Mexico, Arizona, Texas, and California. Thousands who have met him in person know him also as Director of the Bancroft Library and Professor of History at the University of California, one of the most willing and most public-spirited laborers in the great vineyard of history. How much he has given of himself, how creatively he has wrought, will become apparent as time lends perspective to his work.

Tall, thin, blue-eyed, his nordic fair hair now grayed and receding, charged with intellectual curiosity and nervous energy, and possessed of a quick smile and a warming enthusiasm for people and ideas, GPH is at home in many languages, including Spanish and French, Danish and Norwegian, Swedish and German. He comes naturally by this linguistic virtuosity, for he grew up in a family where English and Danish were spoken interchangeably. His father, Niels Peter Jensen Haumann, first saw the light of day in Denmark December 21, 1865. After finishing his army service, as a young man of 24 he voyaged to New York, where he had two uncles in the produce business. Late in 1892, he returned to Denmark to claim Christiane Svendsen as his bride. Following their marriage, February 14, 1893, he brought her to New York. NPJ (he used the initials, and soon followed the example of his uncles in anglicizing his name from Haumann to Hammond) was a farmer at heart. Friends in Minnesota persuaded him to journey on to Hutchinson. There, as the second son in a family of three boys and four girls, George Peter Hammond was born on September 19, 1896.

The Hammonds did not remain long in Minnesota. Even before George's birth, friends taken with "homestead fever" persuaded NPJ to go with them to Ward County, North Dakota, where all staked out claims. GPH's earliest memories are of the flat lands in the vicinity of Kenmare. There much of his boyhood was spent, for he was thirteen years old when the family moved to California.

That move was made because the father had been told he would not survive another Dakota winter; he had contracted typhoid fever while serving in the Danish army, and was never robust afterward. Having friends near Fresno, in October, 1909, he bought raw land at Caruthers, and with his young sons began the labor of building another farm. The age of specialization in California had not yet dawned, so ten acres were planted with alfalfa, ten with peach trees, and the remaining twenty given over to vines. All the family rose early and worked late. Yet the education of the Hammond children was paramount. Caruthers boasted a one-teacher elementary school, but when George reached high school age he had to go each day to Easton, eight miles distant.

At Easton High George was fortunate in coming upon a principal, Mervyn F. Thompson, who was a natural-born teacher, with endless patience for anyone with stars in his eyes. Men like Thompson live for students who devour every printed page they can get their hands on, and it was he who set George's feet upon the path he has trod, inspiring his initial interest in history, and working out his entire college schedule before George presented himself as a freshman at Berkeley in the fall of 1916. (Mervyn Thompson was present when, on April 30, 1963, George acted as master of ceremonies at a reunion of the first thirty classes of Easton High School; then in his eighties, he looked stanch and hale, but died of a stroke a few weeks later.)

At the University of California George majored in history, at first under Henry Morse Stephens and, after Stephens' death, under Herbert E. Bolton. For a time contemporary history in the shape of World War I promised to take charge of his life; George tried unsuccessfully to enlist in the Air Corps, and was drafted by the United States Army. But the date set for induction was November 11, 1918, and after marching in Fresno with some thousands of others, George's military career ended that very day. He graduated with his class at U. C. in 1920, and went on immediately to win his M.A. degree, conferred in May, 1921. The thesis he submitted was "German Interest in California Before 1850."

Soon after attaining his M.A., on August 3, 1921, George married Carrie Nelson, whom he had first met in the Lutheran church at Easton, and who like himself was a graduate of Easton High. Also of Danish ancestry, brown-haired and brown-eyed, with limitless good nature and a wry sense of humor, she was a native of Utah, having been born at Ogden, where her father at the time was a railroad man. Soon after their marriage, early in September, 1921, George and his bride were visited at their home on Benvenue Avenue in Berkeley by his parents and sisters. Returning home, his father was taken ill—having again contracted typhoid fever, it was thought—and died. His mother survived into her ninetieth year, dying at Fresno in 1960.

The acquisition of the Bancroft Library in 1905, followed by the recruitment of Herbert E. Bolton in 1911 as a member of the History Department, had served to orient the University of California in the direction of the Spanish roots of American history, and George looked to this cultural heritage for his Ph.D. thesis. He was attracted by the singular mystery attending the inception of Santa Fe, no one being sure just when the city was founded, or by whom, and it occurred to him that he might investigate the life and times of Don Juan de Oñate, the colonizer of New Mexico. But almost equally appealing was that commanding figure in the maritime history of California, Sebastián Vizcaíno. Finally George made up his mind for Oñate. The choice was fortunate, for despite much combing of archives little more is known of Vizcaíno today than in 1922, whereas the pursuit of Oñate in the Spanish archives opened up a whole new world to scholarship, incidentally establishing GPH in his life work.

Some years earlier, the Native Sons of the Golden West had set up a program to enable promising graduate students at the University of California to pursue researches in foreign archives. When such a fellowship was offered him in the summer of 1922, George seized the opportunity and, with Carrie, sailed for Spain. For a year he labored in the archives at Seville, digging out the basic documents for his study of Oñate. There, also, he became intimately acquainted with that remarkable businessman-turned-scholar, Henry R. Wagner, who was himself prying out of the archives the documents on which he based many subsequent books. As a student employee in the Bancroft Library, George had met Wagner earlier, but not on the same terms. He and Wagner became good friends, and remained so until the redoubtable Henry died in 1957, in his ninety-fifth year.

George returned home to write his thesis, so completing the requirements for the Ph.D. degree, which the University of California conferred upon him in the spring of 1924. This was a homecoming all around, for in that fall of 1923, after a fourteen-year absence, George returned to North Dakota, having accepted an appointment as instructor in American history at the State University. His first publication, "Some Impressions of Spain," appeared almost at once in the *Quarterly Journal* of that institution, a personal narrative in some respects even more interesting today than when written, for it anticipated much of the ensuing history of modern Spain. That article is reprinted in the present volume for the enjoyment of his friends, and for the insight it gives us into the mind and spirit of a very young George P. Hammond, in the process of becoming the GPH so many of us know.

More significant was George's article, "The Desertion of Oñate's Colony from New Mexico," printed in the *Quarterly Journal* for January, 1925, for here was anticipated the appearance of his distinctive thesis, in the first six issues of the *New Mexico Historical Review*, 1926–1927. (The thesis, in 1927, was separately published by the Historical Society of New Mexico as GPH's first book, *Don Juan de Oñate and the Founding of New Mexico*.)

Something else of high importance occurred at Grand Forks. Having become interested in a remarkable narrative penned in Mexico in

1584 by Baltasar Obregón, *Crónica, comentario ó relaciones de los descubrimientos antiguous y modernos de Nueva España y del Nuevo México,* George resolved to publish an English translation. Coming upon a difficult passage, he went around to the Spanish Department for help. The Spanish Department in that year consisted of one man, who had been born in Pontevedra, Spain, on March 24, 1892, migrated to South America and the U. S. A., became a U. S. citizen and obtained his B.S. and M.A. degrees from the University of Michigan in 1921–1922. His name was Agapito Rey. As an assistant professor, he had joined the North Dakota faculty at the same time as George, and they taught there the same two years.

Hammond and Rey proved to be natural collaborators in the translation of early Spanish documents; and the work they began in Grand Forks has profitably continued ever since, though it was to Indiana University that Rey moved in 1925, to remain until his retirement in 1962.

It was anomalous that one of the most promising young scholars in the field of Southwestern history should be operating from a North Dakota base. The University of Arizona perceived the fact, offering George an appointment as assistant professor of history for the year 1925–1926, and promoting him to associate professor the following year. GPH remembers with pleasure the years at Tucson, but his professional horizons were rapidly expanding, and he was happy to accept an appointment to the faculty of the University of Southern California in the fall of 1927.

He remained eight years in Los Angeles, one of the most productive eras of his life. During this time, in 1933, he first visited Mexico on sabbatical leave, spending a happy six months delving in the archives at Mexico City. And he also fairly launched the impressive series of publications relating to Southwestern history with which his name will always be identified.

The springboard was *Obregón's History of 16th Century Explorations in Western America,* the joint work with Rey which was now completed. The book was printed in 1928 by a small Los Angeles firm and the editors ended by paying most of the printer's bills themselves. Not at all discouraged, they went ahead with plans to publish the Luxán narrative of Antonio de Espejo's expedition to New Mexico in 1582–1583. Frederick W. Hodge at the Museum of the American Indian, Heye Foundation, in New York, suggested that if the two young scholars were determined to print the narrative, even at their own expense, they ought to enlarge their ideas, form a society, and print a series on the Southwest he was sure people would buy.

Rey was in far-off Indiana, so George fell to work and wrote up a circular, with Hodge's criticism and advice, announcing a publication program to be carried out by the Quivira Society. At the last moment it became clear that there was a radical defect, in that the Society had no sponsors. Among others, George talked with Wagner, now living in San Marino. Wagner agreed with a laugh to be one of the sponsors, saying with characteristic frankness: "Well, George, there is no harm in giving yourself a name, and publishing a book. If it works, good and well, if not, you can write it off to experience." Other sponsors of the Quivira Society were Arthur S. Aiton, Lansing B. Bloom, Herbert E. Bolton, Charles W. Hackett, Edgar L. Hewett, F. W. Hodge, J. Lloyd Mecham, A. B. Thomas, and of course Hammond and Rey. George P. Hammond appeared as managing editor, with Bolton and Hodge as advisory editors. Thus, in 1929, came forth the first volume of the Quivira Society, in an edition of 500 copies: *Expedition to New Mexico Made by Antonio de Espejo, 1582–1583.* The book was very well received, and in due course was followed by others, including a new edition of Wagner's *The Spanish Southwest.* The Quivira Society eventually issued no less than thirteen publications, all seen through the press by George P. Hammond.

GPH was clearly a phenomenon, having imaginative range, great energy and drive, and a facility for getting things done. The University of New Mexico recruited him for its faculty in 1935, and for eleven years he remained in Albuquerque as Professor of History and head of the department, as well as Dean of the Graduate School. From 1935 to 1938 he served also as Dean of the Upper Division in the College of Arts and Sciences. As though these duties were not enough to keep him busy (and all this time he was publishing books and articles, to say nothing of helping Carrie raise their four children, Frances, Helen, Charles, and George), he acted as State Director for the New Mexico Historical Records Survey, W. P. A., 1936–1939, and during three summers was a visiting professor at various universities. He also served as a member of the U. S. delegation to the 4th Assembly of the Pan-American Institute of Geography and History at Caracas in 1946.

These activities must some day be described in detail—hopefully, by GPH himself. Here we shall concentrate upon another remarkable publishing enterprise. At the time George came to the University of New Mexico, the State was beginning to look ahead to the Coronado Cuarto Centennial, which would come in 1940. The university president, James F. Zimmerman, was a man of large vision who felt that some more lasting benefit should come to New Mexico from the Coronado celebration than the contemplated pageants, delightful as these might be. The suggestion that appealed to him most was GPH's proposal that a Coronado Historical Series be published by the university press. That press had been in a broken-down condition when George came to Albuquerque, but Zimmerman found money for new type and equipment so as to justify printing the later Quivira books in Albuquerque; and the press was beginning to reflect credit on the State and its university.

Again, the story must some day be told in fuller detail, but in May, 1940, the University of New Mexico Press had ready Hammond and Rey's *Narratives of the Coronado Expedition,* first of twelve volumes contemplated for a permanent memorial to the Cuarto Centennial, all to reflect in one way or another New Mexico's majestic Spanish heritage. Some of the authors who originally agreed to contribute to the series died before they could deliver their manuscripts, and various changes had to be made along the way—the usual effect being that GPH had to assume added burdens. Individual volumes have kept on appearing over the years, and the eleventh will soon be published, George's own *The Rediscovery of New Mexico,* with Agapito Rey, once more.

The years in Albuquerque were happy, though the work load was heavy. But in 1946 George was offered the directorship of the Bancroft Library, and a concurrent appointment in the History Department at the University of California. The challenge and the opportunities of such an appointment he could not resist, and he returned to California to take up permanent residence in Berkeley, settling in at a beautiful home on Contra Costa Avenue, overlooking the Bay.

Here let us interject some passages of George's autobiography. While teaching at the University of Southern California in 1930, GPH had sponsored the formation of a history honor society, Alpha Delta Iota, which reflected its founder's activity and energy, and in fact got out a publication in 1932 to which he contributed a foreword. While this publication was in press, the society was accepted as Xi chapter of Phi Alpha Theta, national history fraternity; the truth is, the national organization first became solvent when the vigorous new Southern California chapter brought its hundred-odd dues-paying members into the fold. Five years later, in December, 1937, George (then national president) attended the fraternity's eighth biennial convention in Philadelphia to find the assemblage much exercised over ritual and other formalisms. When he proposed as much more fitting the founding of a scholarly journal, a committee called upon him at his hotel room at 1 a.m., agreeing to underwrite such a journal if he would edit it. Thus was born *The Historian*, the first number of which was dated Winter, 1938. It has been published ever since, at first semi-annually, now quarterly. George served as editor until autumn, 1946, when the pressures of his new Bancroft job led him to print his valedictory.

None of the above is irrelevant to GPH's life and times, but primarily we wish to quote (from the issue dated Spring, 1946) the only personal remarks he ever printed in *The Historian*, which should not stay buried in the files:

"From his chair in the Bancroft Library, at the University of California, your editor looks out upon a landscape far different from that which he left in New Mexico, when he resigned his position as head of the history department and dean of the Graduate School at the University of New Mexico to become director of the Bancroft Library and professor of history at the University of California, Berkeley. In

Albuquerque, there were mountains in the distance, mirages, a wonderfully blue sky, the Sandias bathed in mysterious colors, wide vistas of rolling mesa, or the delightful afternoon summer storms when it thundered, blew, flashed lightning, and seldom rained.

"These qualities of the environment are missing in the San Francisco Bay Area, except for the brown hills—brown under the dry summer sun. Here the sky seems leaden, heavy with a high fog that would lead a visitor to carry his umbrella. The hillsides are covered with playhouses—so they appear from a distance—but upon closer approach they are the lovely Berkeley homes that crawl ever higher up the hillsides with the increase in population. Often the higher rows of houses are hidden in a blanket of 'high fog,' soon to be dispersed by the forenoon sun.

"Yes, it is a far cry from the Sunshine State of the Southwest to the Golden Gate of the Pacific—one leaves the former with regret, but with pleasant memories, and eagerly looks forward to what the future holds in store. . . . "

George had been preceded in administering the Bancroft Library by Frederick J. Teggart, Herbert E. Bolton, and Herbert I. Priestley. The Bancroft had had a semi-independent character over the years but, in a general reorganization of the University Library in 1945, Bancroft was made a principal division of the Main Library, with a defined collecting field. The University had taken pride in the Bancroft Library, as one of its adornments and a continuing attraction to graduate students and other scholars, but on the whole had not found it possible to support the Bancroft Library in a program of active growth. The staff was small, acquisition funds minimal, and quarters inadequate.

All this has been radically changed in the nineteen years George has served as Bancroft's director. On retirement he can contemplate elevation of the Bancroft Library to the highest rank among America's great research institutions. Better, if still cramped, quarters have been found; immense backloads in cataloguing have been effectually attacked; a manuscripts department has been brought into existence; the staff has been greatly enlarged; a sympathetic University administration has consistently provided funds that have enabled Bancroft to bid in the great Americana auctions and to purchase the vital rarities that turn up from time to time; and a Friends' organization has been brought into being to champion the interests of the Library and aid in its growth. In time to come George P. Hammond's vital contributions to the Bancroft Library, and thereby to world scholarship, will be fully appreciated.

As in the past, his activities as Director of the Bancroft Library have been only one aspect of the whole man. He has taught courses in history during all his years since returning to his alma mater; at the same time he has served innumerable institutions and organizations concerned with the history and culture of California and the West, among them The Friends of the Bancroft Library, California Historical Society, Book Club of California, Roxburghe Club, and national, state, and local historical associations. He has addressed historical and library groups the length and breadth of California, and a good many farther removed, all the while moving a continuous flow of books into print.

The University of New Mexico summoned GPH back to Albuquerque in 1954 to confer upon him the honorary degree of Doctor of Laws. The University's citation spoke for all of us, if not saying all that might have been said, in characterizing George P. Hammond:

"For eleven years a teacher and administrator in this University; devoted scholar who for more than a quarter-century has labored arduously in the collection and preservation of historical records relating to Western America; editor of the Quivira Society publications and the Coronado Cuarto Centennial series which have brought him honor and esteem in this country and abroad; enthusiastic historian of the Spanish Southwest, whose writings will have permanent value for all who seek to know and understand the cultural heritage of New Mexico and neighboring areas; prominent bibliophile and kindly gentleman. . . ."

Various aspects of the life of this man, a man at once very simple and extremely complex in character, are explored in the present volume. Many honors have come his way since the June night in Albuquerque when the University of New Mexico opened this particular door upon his future. Subsequently GPH was elected a member of the American Antiquarian Society, and he has been made a fellow of the New Mexico Historical Society, the California Historical Society, and the Society of American Archivists. In September, 1964, the California Historical Society honored him with its Henry R. Wagner Memorial Award, specifically for the completion of his ten-volume *Larkin Papers*, but in recognition also of his long and distinguished service in the cause of history. Two months later the Society of Pan American Culture gave him its Golden Condor Award for his aid to students of Hispano-American culture; and in December, 1964, the Academy of American Franciscan History honored him with the Serra Award of the Americas, "in recognition of his invaluable contributions to Hispanic and Western American studies as Educator, Librarian, Historian." Addresses delivered by J. S. Holliday and France V. Scholes on two of these occasions make a timely contribution to the present book; and GPH will find that his Response to the Academy has not eluded us.

The foregoing account of GPH, much of it written to serve another purpose, is impersonal on the whole, and I should like to speak in my own voice before giving place to other friends and colleagues. I first met GPH casually in March, 1948, introduced to him in his office by Helen Harding (now Mrs. Bretnor) while doing some research in Bancroft at the end of a transcontinental quest. Five years later he came to Salt Lake City to confer with me about problems relating to the Mormon frontier in the Southwest—I had an atrocious cold and could force from my vocal chords little more than a loud squeak, so that the colloquy had its ludicrous aspect. Later in 1953, at his urging, the University of California offered me an appointment in connection with Bancroft's troubled Guide program and, in January, 1954, after getting clear of a research involvement in Washington, D. C., I appeared in Berkeley to be converted into a Bancrofter.

From that time to the present I have been privileged to observe GPH at close range—as a very human being, as a dedicated scholar, as a no less dedicated Director of the Bancroft Library. I have seen at first hand what he has done to transform the Library—I might almost say, to transform it in his own image. With his qualities of imagination, he has had the power to dream greatly; with his ingenuity and persistence, he has also had the power to implement his dreams. Not all of his dreams; there have been profound frustrations for GPH in his work. But he has demonstrated anew that in our society the dreamers are the truly practical men; the nay-sayers are almost always found in the perspective of time to have been impractical, a costly indulgence of our societal myopia. Generations yet unborn will call George P. Hammond's name blessed. Perhaps they will say that he was ahead of his time—just enough ahead of his time.

A Pleasant Dialogue

AGAPITO REY

In 1923 GPH and I converged on Grand Forks, North Dakota, at the beginning of our teaching careers. We were both trying to complete our doctor's degrees while teaching some sixteen hours a week and engaging in other activities. George had his thesis well along, mine was still on the drawing board. The Hammonds were just back from a year in Spain collecting materials at the Archivo de Indias. A California grant had enabled George to take his bride to Spain and get her interested in his work, an interest that has grown with the years.

At the University of North Dakota we had offices on the top floor of the Administration Building. During the summer vacation, the building was declared unsafe. This floor was taken down, and our books and belongings piled together in the gymnasium. When we returned in the fall, there was a scramble to sort out the mess, and everyone took what he thought was his. We belonged to the young faculty group and played volleyball and other games for exercise.

George was writing a thesis on Don Juan de Oñate, the founder of New Mexico. In Spain he had gathered many documents of first importance for this work, and extremely valuable for the study of early Spanish activities in our Southwest. He thought some of these should be published and began the tedious task of transcribing them from the photostat copies. One day George came into my office with a document which troubled him. I agreed to look at it, and found it most interesting. It was a history of Western America written in

13

Mexico in 1584 by Baltasar Obregón. We exchanged a few remarks regarding the document and then some one said, I believe it was George, "Why not work it together?" We did. I transcribed the Spanish text and made an English translation. George checked and polished it, then worked the annotation. This method seemed satisfactory and we followed it in all of our subsequent work. So began a collaboration that has continued for more than forty years, with no end in sight. We have enough work planned to keep us going for quite a while.

Soon after we started our Obregón collaboration, we became interested in Gallegos' narrative of the Chamuscado expedition to New Mexico in 1581–1582, having obtained photostats of the manuscript in the archives at Seville. This work appeared in the *New Mexico Historical Review*, and in a separate volume in 1927, our first work together to appear in print. Our Obregón work was finished, but we did not know how to bring it out.

After two years of frigid winters, we both left North Dakota; George for the University of Arizona in warm Tucson, I for Indiana University, where I remained until retirement in 1962.

Lacking a publisher for *Obregón's History*, we decided to publish it ourselves. A printer in Los Angeles brought it out for us in 1928. We took a bad shellacking. The volume did not move, and to save storage and handling charges we drastically eliminated the excess copies and took our loss. We had no regrets. It was a worth-while experience that served us well later on. I was single then and could absorb the loss, but George had young children to rear. He was not at all concerned; money has never been his god. As for myself, at that very time I helped finance another book being printed in Spain, and fared no better. While we did not do well financially, our work was cordially received and we were greatly encouraged by the critics.

After two years at the University of Arizona, the Hammonds moved to the University of Southern California in Los Angeles. They built a lovely Spanish-type home in the hills, into which they moved in October, 1929. Two years later my wife and I visited them there. By then the Hammond family of two girls and two boys was complete.

After publishing the *Gallegos Relation* and *Obregón's History*, George and I felt we should bring out Luxán's narrative of the Espejo expedition, as these works are intimately related. As we got the volume ready, we began to think of ways and means to get it published. GPH had become acquainted with F. W. Hodge and Henry R. Wagner, distinguished scholars and bibliophiles. Both had published fancy limited editions of some of their works, and we founded the Quivira Society on similar principles, its publications to consist of numbered copies limited to those who subscribed beforehand. George was the prime mover—chief editor, treasurer, and general manager. We had an advisory council, but it was GPH who did the work. We initiated the Quivira publications in 1929 with Luxán's narrative. George worked hard looking for worthy manuscripts, seeing them through the press and doing the editorial and managing work himself. The thirteen volumes that have been published are a tribute to his scholarship and industry. Complete sets of the Quivira volumes are difficult to come by.

In 1935 GPH moved to Albuquerque to become head of the History Department and Dean of the Graduate School at the University of New Mexico. Next year I came to Albuquerque to teach in the summer session and to work with George in our collaborations. He bought a house and moved that summer while the family was away. We transplanted some rose bushes and tomato plants George had set out at his rented quarters. GPH has always been an enthusiastic gardener and raises beautiful flowers—roses in Los Angeles and Albuquerque, now dahlias. By 1941 this house, located on Monte Vista Avenue at what was then the edge of town, needed enlargement for his growing children. This could be done by digging and building a basement apartment for the two boys, and I recall getting some healthful exercise that summer, helping George shovel dirt out of the basement window. During a visit to Albuquerque later, I had the pleasure of occupying these new quarters, beautifully finished—all George's handicraft. He likes to work with his hands and finds relaxation digging in his garden or puttering in the house. He has made many changes in every house he has owned, including his present Berkeley home.

In 1935 the New Mexico legislature created a Coronado Cuarto

Centennial Commission to celebrate the fourth centennial of Francisco Vásques Coronado's exploration of New Mexico in 1540. Clinton P. Anderson, then a prominent local insurance man, later to attain political eminence, became the director of this Commission, which planned to organize a pageant depicting Coronado's *entrada*, to be staged in various cities in the State. It was quite a show. The writer of the script and the producers found it necessary to consult the Spanish documents bearing on the expedition and translate them for use.

GPH was named director of this historical phase of the celebration, and at his instance I was invited to come to Albuquerque for a year as a research associate. I don't remember having any particular title; what pleased me was that George and I could be together again to continue our collaboration. I was provided with an office in the University Library next to his and proceeded to pore over hundreds of photostats already available and many more obtained later. We had a delightful and profitable year and both our families became intimately acquainted.

The Coronado Commission agreed that one feature of the celebration should be the publication of a series relating to the exploration and founding of New Mexico. This was the Coronado Historical Series, of which GPH became chief editor. Twelve volumes were planned covering the New Mexico Spanish period in the sixteenth, seventeenth and eighteenth centuries, entrusted to well-known specialists. George and I undertook to prepare Volume II: *Narratives of the Coronado Expedition*, which came out in the spring of 1940, the first volume to appear. This was a most satisfying collaboration; we were both living in Albuquerque, and since the work was printed by the New Mexico University Press, we were able to see it through the press with a minimum of confusion or delay.

We agreed also to prepare Volume V of the Series, comprising documents relating to the founding of New Mexico by Don Juan de Oñate and we started assembling materials while still working on the Coronado volume. We thought we could finish it in a short time with the other volume out of the way, but it turned out to be a big job that took us ten long years to complete. It came out finally in two large volumes.

The Coronado Commission had set aside an amount of money to publish these volumes as the authors turned in their manuscripts. When the celebration was over, the Commission found it did not have enough funds to meet its obligations. The publication fund was used to pay those debts, leaving the Historical Series high and dry. President Zimmerman, who had been a moving force in the Cuarto Centennial from the beginning, pledged the help of the University of New Mexico Press to bring out the volumes, but there was no money to carry out his noble intentions, and we could foresee endless delays, even the abandonment of the project. George was very much disturbed, as one could well imagine. Here he was, general editor of the Series, with contracts drawn with different authors, unable to guarantee the publication of their works. But GPH has always been resourceful. He discussed the situation with Clinton Anderson, who by now had gone into politics in a big way. Anderson, as Director of the Coronado Commission, had approved some of the publication contracts, and he maintained his interest in the project. Besides, he was a collector of books about the region and well informed on rare imprints. Anderson wanted the publications to proceed without undue delay, so he canvassed some New Mexican industrialists and friends and collected a fund that guaranteed the publication of all the works of the Coronado Series.

George and I always kept several irons in the fire. We had obtained a photostat copy of Alonso de Benavides' Report of 1634, which we found double the size of another report he had written four years earlier. We proceeded to translate it and get it ready for inclusion in the Coronado Series. In 1943 we were ready to go to press. Since F. W. Hodge had profusely annotated the Edward E. Ayer edition of Benavides' 1630 Memorial (1916) we wanted him to join us as the senior partner in publishing the expanded Report of 1634. He agreed, and we used his notes, expanding them and bringing them up to date, making this our most "erudite" work. In 1944 we were able to tap the new publication fund, and next year *Fray Alonso de Benavides' Re-*

vised Memorial of 1634 rolled off the press. Unfortunately the big war was raging and we could not secure paper comparable in quality to that used in the other volumes.

All the while, our Oñate volume continued to grow. First we thought we would select enough documents for a 300-page volume, but we had now materials to fill three volumes that size. This was to have been Volume VI of the Series, to be published in two parts, but since Professor Lansing Bloom had died without doing the work assigned to him, we brought out our *Don Juan de Oñate, Colonizer of New Mexico* in 1953 as Volumes V and VI, thus filling the gap left in the numbers. (Volumes VIII, IX, and X had already appeared.)

Volume III of the Coronado Series, dealing with the New Mexico period between the expeditions of Coronado and Oñate, had been entrusted to Professor Arthur Aiton of the University of Michigan. He too died before preparing the manuscript. It was up to GPH to find a substitute. After canvassing the situation and the prospects of an acceptable replacement, he and I reached the conclusion we would have to produce one ourselves. We had long thought our exhausted editions of the *Gallegos Relation* and Luxán's *Narrative* could stand a good revision. We also thought that Castaño de Sosa's *Memorial* and other documents relating to his unauthorized expedition of 1590 should be made available to the English reader. These works comprise this Volume III, now in press under the title: *The Rediscovery of New Mexico*. That will complete our joint labor up to 1965, comprising only our books done in collaboration, without including a couple of articles we have written together.

Not all our joint works have appeared in print. We have in different stages of completion volumes on Fr. Zárate Salmerón, Arricivita with the life of Fr. Margil de Jesús, a study of Oñate's membership in the Order of Santiago, and Bandini's History of California. We have also been toying with a plan to print in Spain the Spanish texts from which we made our English versions. (Many of these texts have never been published in the original Spanish.) We have enough work on hand to keep us from becoming bored in "retirement." This does not include works in our specialties, done individually, such as the ten-volume

Larkin Papers George has just completed after long years of labor, or my own studies in medieval Spanish literature.

While the Hammonds were in Albuquerque, I came there several summers, to teach or do research on our works. On certain occasions when our families were away, GPH and I used to tour the State to locate and become familiar with Indian pueblos and places encountered in the documents we were studying. George also accompanied Dr. Bolton on a 1940 trip to Mexico to retrace Coronado's route from Compostela.

Since the Hammonds moved to Berkeley nineteen years ago, we have had many occasions to work together again, as I taught several summers at the Universities of Stanford and Southern California, and have also spent extended periods in research at the Bancroft Library. These periods were our most productive, as collaboration and consultation through correspondence tended to slow our work.

I must add here my appreciation to the Hammonds for their splendid hospitality. In my numerous trips to Albuquerque and Berkeley, they insisted I stay at their home. The children doubled up to make room for me, and they all treated me as one of the family.

In our meanderings through New Mexico we, George in particular, were always alert for materials that could be obtained for the University Library. On one occasion we went to the Zuñi area to examine the inscriptions left at El Morro by Oñate and other early explorers; we looked over also the Hawikuh ruins, identified with the glittering "cities" Fray Marcos saw from a distance. We stayed overnight at Ramah, a Mormon town, where we hoped to locate a diary written by an early Mormon settler. We were unsuccessful, but I am sure that George has ever since kept his eye open for such a document.

A most interesting experience was a visit to ex-Governor Otero in Santa Fe. For some time George had been discussing with the patriarch and his wife the ultimate disposition of his papers. At last it was agreed that they be given to the University of New Mexico Library. We drove to the Governor's house one morning and he invited us to stay for lunch, during which we talked about generalities. Governor Otero was then very old, feeble and unsteady on his feet, but his mind was still lucid and he could out-talk and out-drink any of us. At about two o'clock the Governor was ready for a nap and we, for a breath of fresh air. Before retiring, the old man had agreed to let the University carry away his books and papers. His wife added that we could also take the bookcases. Before the day was over, the University trucks were loading up. This is a good example of George's collecting efficiency. Later on, Señor Otero and his family gave the mementos he had acquired during his service in the Philippines and as Governor of New Mexico. I accompanied George on other forays for old papers, both in New Mexico and California, and have always admired his patience and persistence. His success in these activities is easily discernible in the Bancroft Library acquisitions during his administration.

Now that George goes into "retirement," as I have been for the last three years, we may be able to put new sparkle into our collaboration and complete some long-dormant projects. We have both enjoyed our more than forty years of friendly association. We look back bemused to our first meeting in Grand Forks, North Dakota, never dreaming then that our pleasant dialogue would last so long.

Bancroft, Old and Ever New

CHARLES L. CAMP

During fifty-three years of association with the University of California I have known all the leaders in the activities of the Bancroft
Library, and have enjoyed the privilege of research in those rich
sources of our history. The person chiefly responsible for the purchase of the Library, Professor Henry Morse Stephens, was my first
teacher in history at this University. He had a forceful personality,
was a vigorous lecturer and remains an inspiration largely, I think,
because of his breadth and perspective. He "covered" the history of
the Western World in a year's lectures, and had able teaching assist-
ants—mine was John J. Van Nostrand whose section dealt with the
Athenians. Charles Edward Chapman was another of Stephens' teaching fellows.

Professor Stephens had been invited to the University by President
Benjamin Ide Wheeler, and Stephens had a profound influence. It was
he who induced Wheeler and the University of California to purchase
the Bancroft Library, despite the cynical comments and criticisms of
Ambrose Bierce and others. Stephens obtained letters from prominent
historians, one of whom, Reuben Gold Thwaites, recommended that
the Library, when purchased, be "separately administered." Difficul-
ties were encountered in raising the purchase price, and Bancroft
himself came to the rescue with a substantial donation.

Bancroft's prodigious and persistent collecting activities had ceased
by 1895. The library was then housed in a solid, cubical brick build-

21

ing at 1580 Valencia Street in San Francisco. Besides the precious manuscripts, maps and newspapers, it contained some 60,000 books. Miraculously, it escaped the fire of 1906, and the University made haste to remove it to Berkeley only a month after that disaster.

The fire destroyed the famous library of the Mechanics Institute, the San Francisco Public Library, half of the Sutro Library, the greater part of the Library of the Society of California Pioneers, the records of the State Surveyor General, and the entire Hall of Records. Bancroft foresightedly had made abstracts of much of the historically valuable material in those libraries.

Frederick J. Teggart had been the librarian of the Mechanics Institute. When that library was destroyed, he was called to superintend the removal of the Bancroft collection to Berkeley. He then became the Bancroft's first honorary custodian. He began the cataloguing of the collection and engaged some of Morse Stephens' graduate students to labor on the transfer of the collection to the top floor of the new California Hall at Berkeley. There the mass of material lay on temporary shelving until the Doe Library building was completed in 1911. All of the Bancroft was then moved into the large room 100, now the Periodical Room and Stacks, to the left of the main entrance on the first floor of Doe.

Meanwhile Professor Stephens had brought in Herbert Eugene Bolton (from Texas by way of Stanford), and installed him in the History Department. He became Acting Curator and finally the first Director of the Bancroft succeeding Professor Teggart whose title had become "Curator." Bolton's "Librarian" was Herbert Ingram Priestley. And Priestley was in charge when I first visited the Library. He had already a good working knowledge of the collection. When you requested a book he would go to the two folio volumes that contained Bancroft's original listings (known in the Library today as the "Valencia Street Catalog"). He seemed in some mysterious way to know where to find your book, and was not too busy to attend to the requests of a lowly freshman.

I slipped into history through the back door. After Stephens' course, I never returned to that department. But I wanted to trace out the explorations made by naturalists in the West, and the Bancroft Library was the source of stirring narratives.

When I came back to the University with my Ph.D. in 1922, the Bancroft staff was busy moving the collections to the "attic" floor of the Doe Library on the Campanile side of the building. This was an inconvenient place to get into. Teggart had by that time graduated from the Department of History to his own private Department of Social Institutions. He had of course been on the team that Stephens organized—the Academy of Pacific Coast History—and had edited a number of diaries and other Western narratives. He finally took up a study of the causes of war, only to admit to bafflement in respect to a common denominator on that subject.

To return to Bolton, I came to know him well. He was blunt and outspoken, had no restraints. His office was along the narrow corridor near the southeast corner of the Bancroft area of the Doe Library. On the door he posted a sign: "Idle persons and chatterers, Keep Out!" At the time of Bolton's retirement, Priestley substituted another sign, obtained, it is rumored, by bribing a Pullman porter—"Quiet is requested for those who have retired."

The interior of Bolton's office was piled high with books, maps, diaries, papers, even unanswered and probably unopened letters. His rule was that if you left a letter long enough it would either answer itself or no longer need an answer. The Professor would be there, busy with his manuscripts, a cigarette in his mouth and a mass of half-burned stubs spilling out of his ash tray. He wrote rapidly and fluently, seldom more than a paragraph to a page. He could then reorganize without wasting time in copying. If books were missing from the Library, the first place to search would be in Bolton's office. He took stacks of books home and would read them in bed until all-hours in the morning.

His conversation was vigorous, rapid, with full-arm gestures as in his lectures, and enthusiastically detailed when describing his own research. He and I used to attend the California Historical Society meetings together, and he was the only member of the history department to do so at that time. One result was that he obtained the interested and fruitful support of a generous Director of the Society, Sidney M. Ehrmann, in financing the publication of his great works on Palou, Anza and Font.

Bolton was geographically minded and loved to retail his experiences in following the tracks of such pioneers as Escalante and Kino. He even made a hazardous voyage down the Colorado, intersecting Escalante's trail at the "Crossing of the Fathers" in Glen Canyon. When I went to Sonora, he told me what to visit; and the location of the earliest seventeenth century Kino Mission, where I picked up some adobe bricks to be melted down for weed seeds for Professor George Hendry, of Agronomy.

Clarence John DuFour had written a thesis on Fort Ross under Bolton's direction. He had promised this manuscript to us for an issue of the California Historical Society Quarterly (September, 1933) that we were getting out, on the "Russians in California." DuFour told me: "If you can get it from Bolton's office, you can have it." He had evidently tried that before.

I cornered Professor Bolton one day, and he promised to look up the DuFour item and send it to us. Some weeks went by. I saw Bolton again and he snapped his fingers and declared that he would send it right over. Still no manuscript. Finally he led me into his office on a prospecting tour. He started at one end and I dismantled a tall stack in the opposite corner. At the very bottom of my pile—there was Clarence DuFour's thesis.

Bolton had a wonderful good humor, could give and take without offense. He asked me one day: "Camp, why are you dabbling in history, why don't you stick to your field?"

I replied: "History is my field. You should know that paleontology is the best kind of history. It has not been warped by the distortions of the written records."

Bolton, Priestley, and Chapman charged across the Western Hemisphere as if on a polo field. Bolton, especially, spread himself over the Spanish frontier from Florida to the Southwest. He was absolutely tireless. After retirement at seventy he was recalled to teach during World War II. With all this excitement going on, some thought that not enough attention was being paid to the American period of Western history. But Bolton had a small army of students doing research in every direction; and some of these, Roy Hafen and Joseph J. Hill among others, have done more than their share on the "American" scene.

Henry Raup Wagner and Herbert Bolton were good friends, though mildly critical of each other. Wagner's idea in reorganizing the California Historical Society was partly to stimulate interest in fields that he thought were being slighted by the History Department and the Bancroft staff. The Society was pretty strictly amateur, and not taken too seriously by the professionals; nevertheless Bolton showed an active interest and cooperated. When the Drake Plate of Brass was discovered, Wagner thought that Bolton had gone off half-cocked in his enthusiasm and suggested further investigations, which were eventually performed. The Plate rests in the Bancroft today through the interest and support of members of the Historical Society. It would be difficult now to reconstruct the history of the Plate of Brass —and inappropriate to go into the petty antagonisms engendered. Bolton and Wagner were both too large in spirit to permit any such emotions to mar their friendship.

Wagner independently worked in the Archives of the Indies in Seville, which so many of the Fellows of the Native Sons of the Golden West had ploughed, and were still ploughing. Those fellowships had been organized by Morse Stephens, and in Wagner's day one of the recipients was George Hammond. In Seville a friendship developed between Wagner and Hammond which was to have an important influence in the later appointment of George Hammond as Bancroft's Director.

Robert Ernest Cowan, San Francisco bookseller, book collector and virtuoso, was of course an early member of the Historical Society. His renowned work on the Bibliography of California became a guide for collecting in that field. A stinging review of the work by Professor Priestley created a rift between the two which Cowan's quick Irish temper kept alive to the end. Nevertheless, some of Cowan's collections of books and manuscripts are a pride of the Library today.

Professor Bolton became Curator of the Bancroft Library in 1916, Director in 1920 and again in 1944. Priestley was named Associate Curator in 1912, Librarian in 1920, and Director upon Bolton's retirement in 1940. He died, after suffering a cerebral stroke, in 1944. Mrs. Eleanor Ashby Bancroft (no relation to H.H.) became Assistant to Priestley in 1940, and until her death in 1956 similarly served Hammond. She had a remarkable knowledge of the collections, and was of immense help to those who worked in the library. She is remembered with deep affection and admiration.

Professor Priestley was not so colorful a figure as Bolton. Physically the two men were similar, about the same build, height and weight. Priestley appeared to be much more reserved, quieter, not so outgoing. He was deeply concerned with the welfare of his students and would defend them against exploitation. He had a well-developed sense of humor and took delight in the peculiar initiation ceremonies of E Clampus Vitus when he was inducted into that hilarious assemblage in the Miwok round house at Tuolumne. He was pleasant, personable, and good looking, except for his one sightless eye. This never disturbed anyone after the first meeting.

I think of George Hammond today most affectionately as one of my closest friends. I do not remember having met him before he came in as Director. But his fame as an historian and editor of the Quivira Society publications had gone on before him. He has enjoyed a host of friends and well wishers. He has devoted himself single-mindedly to the interests of the Bancroft, organized the "Friends," and attracted varied donors. He has carried on important editorial and research programs, built up the collections (notably microfilm), inspired and retained the devotion of an increasing staff. The Library has been fortunate; under his directorship it has come to serve broad public needs, as well as the immediate interests of the University.

When I arrived at the University in 1911, the Library was migrating from Bacon Hall to the Doe Memorial building, then the most imposing and commodious structure on the campus. Its vast inner spaces seemed more than ample, yet scarcely five years passed before extensive alterations and additions had to be planned. An early thought envisaged spreading into arboretum glade directly north of the Library and connecting that area with the Doe building by an underground passageway. Another idea was to take over Wheeler Hall. The present Annex was the answer. That addition would scarcely be recognized today as a new structure, so neatly is it integrated with the old. The miles of shelf space required for the yearly acquisitions baffled the architects, and they suggested an expansible, factory-type of building that could be indefinitely enlarged. This has so far been avoided by using warehouse space for little-circulated materials, and by spreading collections into specialized libraries elsewhere on the campus.

Since 1950 the Annex has housed the Bancroft Library. It had been suggested that the Bancroft be moved to old Boalt Hall—that, by now, would have become inadequate. It was also hoped that a separate new building would be provided for Bancroft. Time has demonstrated the interdependence of the two Libraries and it would be a mistake to separate them widely.

The Annex occupies the site of an historic structure, old North Hall, a relic of the original University setup—antedated only by the more sturdy South Hall, which still stands. North Hall was for years the main University classroom building. It had a bell, seldom rung, in the superstructure, and the entire complex of the Student Store lay in its narrow basement. Senior Bench, crudely mutilated by the initials of future senators and statesmen, no doubt, stood next to the entrance of the store. It was the social center for gossip and banter— off limits to all Co-eds, and occupied only by the Stetson-hatted Seniors. It stood very close to what is now the main entrance to the Bancroft. That was where the steep stairway went up to the first floor of North Hall, and how those shaky old floors would quiver between classes!

Bacon Hall, until 1963, occupied the space where Birge Hall now stands. In its day it was a model, designed not only as a library but also to house a singular collection of art treasures including some heroic statuary representing Ariadne sitting on an unhappy looking panther. The book stacks were located in the rotunda and on the upper circular gallery under the glass dome. The book cases were of polished black-walnut with glass doors above and larger shelves below. These wonderful cases were transferred to various offices after the books were removed. I had some in later years, and they can still be found on the campus as well as in a book store on Oxford Street, where they look just as sturdy and handsome as they did fifty years ago.

Bacon Hall had another claim to fame. I have been told it was one of the first buildings in the East Bay wired for electric lights, and that visitors came just to see this phenomenon. The ground floor was a series of dungeon-like caverns where members of the geology department later had their offices, leaving the more open spaces above to house collections. The upper galleries were inhabited by the fossils and offices of the Museum and Department of Paleontology. Cracks in the dome created shower baths in those quarters during storms.

It was something of a mystery how the great University library could ever have been contained in Bacon Hall. After it was taken out, Harold Leupp said he was sure he could never have put the books back there again.

Mr. Leupp was the second University librarian, following the venerable Joseph Cummings Rowell. Rowell stayed on long after his retirement, a white-haired veteran who continued to work away. He had built up the library from small beginnings. He had organized the archives collection, and he wrote out the original catalogue cards and labeled the volumes with his own hands. Under him, important bequests were secured, such as the Reese fund.

Harold Leupp was an efficient librarian, a stickler for rules and order. He saw to it that Case "O" was kept securely locked in his own office, and he had the only key. It was rumored that he sometimes took a peek himself, but he didn't allow his secretaries into that sanctum. He and I and "Captain" Kidd of Boalt Hall used to play handball together. It was remarkable how young he looked even after he was 60. He retained the smooth complexion and physique of a boy. After his "retirement" he went to the San Francisco Presidio as a book buyer for their library. He died in 1952 at the age of 75. He was a man of varied interests and attainments, particularly in the knowledge of English literature.

The history of an institution is bound to be interesting to those who have seen it evolve. Such a remarkable institution as the Bancroft Library deserves careful attention. These itinerant notes may add a mite to the more detailed surveys of the future.

I never knew or even saw Hubert Howe Bancroft. One aspect of the career of this great historian is particularly remarkable—his amazing ability as a collector of books and manuscripts. If he had never written a word of history, Bancroft would be forever in our country's debt for collecting and preserving the rapidly vanishing records of our history. Whatever may be thought of the literary quality of the Bancroft volumes—and that quality varies with the different authors—they constitute an almost incredibly detailed bibliographic key and abstract of sources. And most of these sources stand available to students, in the Bancroft collections.

A Time of Adventure

ROBERT H. BECKER

The Bancroft Library has meant a great deal to many people during its six decades at the University of California, and there are among its present staff and patrons a goodly number who recall with nostalgia the "Bolton Years," when the Library and its Director, Herbert E. Bolton, were the focus for a remarkable amount of finished research and a still more remarkable number of fledgling scholars. The image provoked in reminiscence is that of a casual, slap-happy place, terribly overcrowded and sadly understaffed, a place where books and manuscripts were piled on the floors for lack of shelf-space, and if the thing you were looking for wasn't in one pile, it just might be in the next.

Under the circumstances, the Library and its staff were doing the best they could. Consider that in 1938 the Library was manned by only three full-time employees apart from Professors Bolton and Priestley, Director and Librarian respectively, who besides administering the Library were carrying full teaching loads in the Department of History! The total budget allocated to Bancroft during that year was $11,640, including $2,500 for the purchase of books. Moreover, the passage of time did not seem to improve matters.

World War II brought with it a reduction in funds for the operation of the entire University, and with it the Bancroft Library. For three years, no money at all could be found for the purchase of books, and in 1946 the staff consisted of only four people, including Director

Emeritus Bolton, who had returned as interim administrator of the Library after the untimely death of Professor Priestley in 1944.

The Bancroft Library was at a crossroads when George Hammond became its Director in the summer of 1946. An Old Bancroft Hand, having worked in the library as a student assistant while still an undergraduate, and having taken his Doctorate under Professor Bolton in 1924, GPH knew the immense potential, the unexploited richness in the collections, and he had assurance from both President Robert Gordon Sproul and University Librarian Donald Coney of increased support for the Bancroft's programs.

George P. Hammond was even then a man wise in the ways of universities. After a period of settling in, he could see many improvements that might be made, especially in the invigorating post-war climate of expansion, but he also knew the value and force of external leverage. An outside expert was likely to be listened to more attentively than the man on the job. Therefore, acting on the historic precedent of 1905, when Dr. Reuben Gold Thwaites was brought to Berkeley to give counsel on the proposed purchase of the Bancroft Library, he persuaded the University authorities to commission a report by the distinguished scholar, Dr. Roscoe R. Hill, a famous Latin-Americanist then occupying a responsible post in the National Archives. Dr. Hill's report and recommendations singularly coincided with GPH's private views, though that may prove no more than that he too could recognize the logic of facts, and the consequences that should flow from them. At any rate, Hill's report, submitted to President Sproul in the summer of 1947, set up guidelines that have influenced the development of Bancroft ever since.

"The visitor to the Bancroft Library," Dr. Hill noted, "is immediately impressed by two outstanding facts. First, the extensive and extremely valuable character of the collection; and second, the crowded conditions in which the materials are housed. Moreover, if the visitor is an investigator he soon realizes that as yet proper and adequate tools for securing access to the rich treasures had not been prepared. . . ." In short, the Library needed those two items essential to any significant research collection: space and people. Space was already planned for, through new construction. People would have to wait until there was room for them to work. In the meantime, and in spite of the overcrowding, there could be a beginning. The Director hired a secretary; he had been typing his own letters!

The Hill Report pointed up the necessity for establishing order in the Library's vast collection of manuscripts, an undertaking that could be carried out properly only by someone with training and experience. And such a person soon appeared, as GPH has recalled:

"Late in 1947, a handsome young University of California Alumna (Class of '20 like myself) called at the Bancroft Library and inquired about a job. She was especially trained in the care of manuscripts, was very earnest and sincere, and hoped there would be such an opening. She and her husband were leaving southern California, where she had worked in the Huntington Library, and were returning to Berkeley to make their home here once again. I replied, honestly but discouragingly, that there was no manuscripts department or staff in the Bancroft Library, though we needed one very badly, and that there was no budget, no money for a new appointment. When the young lady said she cared more about a job than money ... I sighted a faint glimmer of hope. The hope became a reality, a position was created, and Mrs. Julia Hamilton Macleod became the first member of a new department in the Bancroft Library—whose entire staff then numbered only seven regular members, including the director, who taught a couple of courses in the History Department."

The Director and Mrs. Macleod agreed that she should begin by studying the manuscript collection as a whole, with a view to establishing a pattern of cataloguing that would retain as much as possible of Hubert Howe Bancroft's original system, and yet allow for an unlimited intake of new material. Also, a new inventory would be compiled—the first in many years. Working with the Director and his extraordinary assistant, the late Eleanor Ashby Bancroft, Mrs. Macleod devised a system that has fully met the needs of the Library and its patrons from that time to the present. Since 1948, every group of manuscripts then in the Library, and all received subsequently, have been numbered systematically, and their contents briefly described, so that even those collections not yet fully analyzed can be located and used. The entire manuscript collection, estimated at over 1,000,000 units, is now under adequate control, and more than two-thirds of Bancroft's holdings have been processed and made fully available for use.

In commenting on a plan for future acquisitions, Dr. Hill pointed out that in the future it would be impossible to obtain any appreciable amount of original source material from the Latin American countries within Bancroft's collecting field, because the respective countries have taken effective legal measures to prevent the export of their historical documents. Dr. Hill suggested that photographic reproductions of documents, particularly from the archives of Mexico and Spain, might be obtained at reasonable cost.

Not surprisingly, GPH had already considered this idea; in fact, he had formally proposed such a project to President Sproul a few weeks earlier:

"It is my judgment that the most vital, long-range program for the Bancroft Library is the microfilming of documents in foreign archives relating to early California and Latin America. Scholars have 'nibbled' at this program for many years, beginning with Chapman's studies in the archives of Spain. Most of the documents gathered were handwritten, typed, or copied by the small Leica camera. Virtually all of this work was performed by methods now recognized as in the 'horse and buggy' stage. Modern technological developments in the reproduction of documents have been so great that it is now possible to copy thousands of pages by microfilm in the same time that a few pages could be copied previously."

The idea excited immediate interest, as the forward-looking kind of activity a great institution like the University of California should engage in, and money was found as a "special appropriation" to begin the project. Through the help of GPH's old friend Clinton P. Anderson, by that time Secretary of Agriculture, the influence and muscle of the Federal government, particularly the State Department, was enlisted to open channels to the proper authorities in the foreign governments. In order to insure a satisfactory beginning, the Director himself went to Spain in 1949 to initiate the filming there. Afterward, representatives from Berkeley organized filming programs in other countries, notably Professor Woodrow Borah in Mexico, Dr. Gwendolin Cobb in Portugal, and Drs. Robert Burke and Roland Duncan in England. The immensity of the project is such that it still continues. The Library can now make available to scholars more than 4,000,000 pages of source material otherwise to be found only in London, Lisbon, Seville, or Mexico City.

Research is, of course, the very reason for being of such a library as Bancroft. But the product of that research, the new ideas or the modification of old ones, the re-evaluations and re-interpretations in the light of previously unknown data, is itself comparatively valueless without dissemination—by means of a program of publication.

Shortly after the purchase of the Bancroft Library by the University, an Academy of Pacific Coast History was organized, its chief function the sponsoring of publications based on the Bancroft Collection. With the death of Professor Henry Morse Stephens in 1919, this effort languished. Director Herbert Bolton produced an impressive number of scholarly works, using the Bancroft Library's holdings, but the pressing need was a series of guides and calendars to the Bancroft Collection itself. This need was reiterated in the Hill Report, and simultaneously with the institution of the Foreign Microfilm Program began a concerted effort to make the Library's holdings better known and more accessible. At first, it was thought that a series of published guides to individual manuscript collections would suffice, but as time went on, it became apparent that such compilations were not enough, that the primary goal should be a guide to the entire manuscript holdings of the Library, though the first idea should not be entirely abandoned. Through the efforts of Mrs. Macleod, Dr. Doris Marion Wright, and especially the Director, a *Guide to the Mariano Guadalupe Vallejo Documentos para la Historia de California*, (*1780–1875*), was published in 1953 as the first of the specialized finding aids.

With the experience gained, the staff began the compilation of an over-all guide to the manuscript holdings. The project went forward under Dale L. Morgan, working closely with Mrs. Macleod, and by

1963 the Library could publish the first volume of the *Guide to the Manuscript Collections of the Bancroft Library*, describing items relating to Canada, Alaska, Hawaii and the Pacific Islands, and all the western States except California. Volume II, describing manuscripts concerned with Mexico and Colonial Spanish America, compiled by Dr. Gwladys Williams has been edited by Dr. Hammond (to be published soon). Califonia manuscripts are described in a volume now in course of preparation. Throughout the period 1948–1964, the Director himself was editing for publication the Library's collection of the papers of Thomas O. Larkin, pioneer California merchant and United States Consul, a monumental contribution to the history of America, as Dr. J. S. Holliday makes clear on a later page.

In 1961 the Bancroft Library Publications Fund was initiated through a generous donation by Mr. and Mrs. Richard Y. Dakin in memory of their daughter, Sara Hathaway Dakin, a promising young writer who died earlier that year at the age of 22. The Fund, augmented by subsequent donations, will enable the Library to maintain a systematic program of publication: guides and calendars; original documents; and scholarly monographs. In fact, money from this Fund enabled the Library and the University Press to produce the first volume of the invaluable *Guide to the Manuscripts Collection* at a price that scholars, researchers, and small libraries could afford.

For many years, although the Library had been the recipient of occasional private funds, sustained support was provided only by the University until the Friends of the Bancroft Library, organized in 1946, gave it a new kind of public backing. The membership roll of the Friends has been a distinguished one, and their contributions in both money and effort have brought to the Library rare books, manuscripts of great distinction, and most recently, in the pictorial field, the Robert B. Honeyman, Jr. Collection. By their active interest, the Friends stimulated support from the University itself in the purchase of the Honeyman Collection through employment of private University funds, voted by the Regents, which amounted to $263,000— slightly more than half of the total price of $550,000.

The Bancroft Library of 1965 is a far different institution from that of 1945. That difference owes primarily to the energy and persistence of its Director, GPH. Fundamental changes were instituted even before the move to the Annex in 1950. By that year, the staff had increased (a little beyond living space), the acquisitions budget had grown from nothing to $10,000, the Foreign Microfilm Project operated with a full-time director in Europe, the chaos in the manuscript collection was yielding to systematic cataloguing and the guide program, and the Friends of the Bancroft Library was a growing, ever more effective organization.

Much of the foregoing I have had to recite from the formal record, for I did not join the staff until 1951 when the years of change were giving way to the years of development. Looking back, I can see that the pattern had been established, the show put on the road, and there was an excitement in the air, as if we were setting out to explore a newly discovered frontier.

It was several months after the Library moved into the Library Annex that I received the call to join its staff—the call was not loud, but I would have heard it had it been the merest whisper, for I had used the Library while a student in the School of Librarianship, and had made up my mind that this, or a library like it, was the place for me. I became a Bancroft reference librarian with training in library techniques and little else, for my undergraduate courses at the University of Oregon were wholly in European History, and my graduate work at Berkeley was in English History, eighteenth-century England at that. My family background included a happy-go-lucky greatuncle who came to western Washington in the 1850's, and I had been sadly overexposed as a child to stories of Ezra Meeker and the Romance of the Oregon Trail. All I could offer really was a burning enthusiasm for the Bancroft Library. I like to think that GPH sensed this feeling when he gave me an interview, and hired me because of it.

At any rate, hired I was, a member of the new Public Services division, under Dr. John Barr Tompkins. It was a time of growth and experimentation, and above all I remember GPH's enthusiastic approval of new ideas for giving better service to the patrons, and making the Library's resources more available. What impressed me then, and still does, was his ability and willingness to put the interest of the Library ahead of his own, rather than the reverse, as is so often the case. GPH was a scholar of the American Southwest, particularly its Hispanic beginnings, but he devoted a great deal of effort to building the Library into a great repository of the records of modern political history; he needed no more than a suggestion from Dr. James D. Hart of the Department of English to begin an impressive collection of manuscripts and papers of literary figures of the West. He recognized the growing importance of pictorial records, giving the responsibility for the formation and indexing of such a collection to Dr. Tompkins.

It is interesting to note the wide variety of acquisitions reported by the Library in, for example, 1948:

The diaries and papers of Mary Atkins, founder of Benicia Seminary, the forerunner of Mills College.

The field notes and correspondence of William Brewer, associated with Josiah Whitney in the first Geological Survey of California.

Thirteen boxes of transcribed documents from the Spanish Archives, relating to Cuba.

Eighty volumes of scrapbooks containing newspaper clippings relating to U.S. Senator James D. Phelan.

Correspondence and business records of the Union Sugar Company for the Betteravia Plant in Santa Barbara County.

A substantial purchase of Mormon materials from the great collection of Herbert S. Auerbach of Salt Lake City.

A large collection of diaries, field notes, manuscripts, photographs, sketches, and other materials covering the anthropological studies of Frans Blom in Central America and Mexico, 1919–1935.

Twenty-five volumes of minutes of the Board of Aldermen, San Francisco, 1852–1855.

Every subsequent report of the major acquisitions shows similar variety.

The years of development—the whole decade of the 1950's—were a most exciting time. There was so much to be investigated, to look at, to wonder about, to work on, that every day became an adventure. GPH made us feel that the Library was *ours,* and I am sure that if he had had the time, he would have turned into as avid a snooper as the rest of us. Throughout the Library, he encouraged a spirit of experimentation, and an awareness of the need for thoughtful innovation and improvement. We made mistakes; some of our experiments were dismal failures; hot projects suddenly went cold. But we learned, always with the conviction that ours was a great library and we would make it a greater one: GPH and all the rest of us.

History Before It Cools

ROBERT E. BURKE

These days, alas, I usually see George Hammond only once or twice a year. But never without recalling the eventful years I spent as one of GPH's Bancrofters. Although the Spanish Borderlands he knows so well are not now, and never have been, one of my major interests, I learned a good deal from George that has nothing whatever to do with "fields." I have come to think of the words "energy" and "Hammond" as synonymous, for he epitomizes, as does no one else I have ever encountered, sheer drive and force in the service of scholarship. Surely all his friends know what I mean, and they will agree with me that he has managed to couple with this energy more than his share of affability. That is not the most prevalent of human qualities, and I wish that more of us had something like George's supply of it; life would be more rewarding for us all.

I first met GPH in 1949, when the papers of former Governor Culbert L. Olson came to the Bancroft Library. In the previous year I had convinced the governor that I was the man to do justice to his hectic and ill-fated administration in a doctoral dissertation. (Later on, I learned that the governor came to wish I had tempered my justice with mercy, but that's another story.) My research project had brought the Olson Papers safely across the Tehachapi—away, that is, from the clutches of Lawrence Powell at UCLA. GPH was glad to see a modern political collection come into the library, and I remember his telling me—after Julia Macleod and Eleanor Bancroft had brought me in to meet him—that it was one of his ambitions to revive the Hubert Howe Bancroft tradition of "collecting history while it was still warm."

I had not been an "Old Bancrofter" (defined in my day as an habitué of the fourth floor of the old library), since the research for my M.A. had been largely statistical and centered in the much-less-glamorous Bureau of Public Administration. Despite my rather shaky credentials, GPH began to take an interest in my work. Sometime in the spring of 1950, as my dissertation moved toward completion, I found that GPH had been checking up on me with my mentor, Professor John D. Hicks. Soon afterward—he is clearly what used to be called a "fast mover"—GPH told me that there was a chance he would have a new job in his budget and asked if I would like to join his staff, with the special task of building the modern manuscripts collections. Having recently emerged from a bruising job-interview with the president of one of the lesser California state colleges, I accepted this tentative offer with what now seems to have been considerable haste. But I still recall the ecstasy of that moment, and if I continue to look upon George as my deliverer, perhaps I can be excused.

As things turned out, GPH had no regular job for me in 1950, but he managed to hire me, just the same. For the most glorious year I have ever enjoyed, I was "Director of the Bancroft Library Research Project in England." By a wonderful combination of circumstances (can it be that one of the secrets of GPH's success is that he knows how to combine circumstances?), he had contrived to secure a State appropriation for foreign microfilming. Recently he had learned that in England were important manuscripts relating to the West, which we might arrange to microfilm. As soon as my dissertation was finished, he arranged a crash on-the-job training program in microphotography for me, and I found myself on the *Queen Mary* bound for Southampton.

For a whole year, I "directed" a staff of two photographers, spending most of my time uncovering business records of British firms active in the West and Mexico for them to film. I negotiated with the Public Record Office for the microfilming of Foreign Office diplomatic and consular papers, dickered with Customs, the Home Office, and Ministry of Labour—what a job it was to be a director even of such a minuscule staff! During all this George Hammond was my faithful Berkeley correspondent, as well as my long-distance boss. My detailed report went off every Saturday, and sometimes I wrote in between. George replied to every point I ever raised. And, since this was my first trip to Europe, and England in 1950–1951 was still marked by Austerity and Controls, I had a good many requests to make. But GPH was not going to let our venture fail if he could help it—and he made life as pleasant as he could for his protegé. Thanks in large measure to the help from home base, we got a lot of microfilm. When I returned to Berkeley in the fall of 1951, I could turn over the project to my successor, Roland E. Duncan, in good running order.

Meanwhile, GPH had secured the budget line, and I returned to become "Head of the Manuscripts Division of the Bancroft Library." (George always has been able to come up with a resounding title when the occasion called for it.) The next five years were not so exciting for me as the English *annus mirabilis,* but there was plenty to do. This is not the place for a full-scale memoir, but I would like to say something about three of our joint ventures—our television series, our collection of political papers, and our involvement with literary manuscripts.

"California Notebook" was the name of our twice-a-week, eight-week-long series on KRON-TV in May and June, 1952. Well-meaning friends in the Office of Public Information, aware that University of California Extension Service had a small budget for experimental educational television, persuaded us that the Bancroft Library was a perfect subject for a series they could produce on a shoestring. Having photogenic eyebrows, I became what is euphemistically known in the TV game as "a host." I had to be on *each* program; George got off easy, since he was able to watch several of the programs in the quiet of his living room. But we worked together, while our producer-friends hovered about, telling us what would photograph, and trying to work in as many facets of the library as they could. On each program we had a guest, generally a person making his TV debut. It was an exciting business to see if the guest could re-

member his pseudo ad libbed lines in any sort of sequence. For our
producer-friends kept one camera on some library rarity, and woe
unto us if the guest happened to refer to the Breen diary just as the
camera zoomed in on a Sutter letter. (Or it would have been woe unto
us if anyone other than our friends had been watching.) The nicest
thing said about our spectacular efforts was the comment by Mrs.
Donald Coney: we were "the best program on the air at that time of
the morning." GPH and I can claim to be pioneers of Bay Area television, but he is doubtless glad we came out of the endless script-
writing and the incessant rehearsals with some sanity left.

I would like to emphasize the breadth of George's collecting interests. I believe that he wanted, more than anything, to be a reincar-
nation of H. H. Bancroft—the collector Bancroft, rather than the
publisher, I hasten to add. Tirelessly and patiently he explained to the
many who seemed convinced that California history stopped a century ago—and who firmly believed that all since then was a sort of
vacuum vaguely occupied by rather dull "current events"—that the
great Bancroft had collected materials of his own recent past and of
what can only be termed "current history." Bancroft quit when his
own books were published, but clearly he expected others to carry on
his work. I believe that GPH felt that he was resuming Bancroft's in-
terrupted collecting when he appointed to his staff—and encouraged
—a man chiefly interested in California's twentieth century.

We picked up a number of modern political collections during my
five years in the library, and laid the groundwork for more acquisition
in the future. The most important achievement was, of course, the
purchase of the elusive Hiram Johnson Papers, perhaps the single most
significant manuscript collection of post-1849 California. I would like
to emphasize that the Director of the library where this major archive
now reposes was the world's foremost authority on *colonial New
Mexico*. If I have never since been much impressed with the phrase
"out of my field," I think that George Hammond is largely responsible.

Even farther afield was the collecting of literary manuscripts. The
library had long had such papers, but neither Hubert Howe Bancroft
nor his successors had made systematic attempts to gather them. The

impetus for our drive came from Professor James D. Hart of the Department of English. For several years it was my pleasure, as George's deputy, to work closely with Hart while we built collections of the papers of Frank Norris, Gertrude Atherton, Jack London, and many others. We sought, with George Hammond's blessing and encouragement, to establish the fact—as if it really *needed* to be established— that literary history is part of all history, and that all the history of the West was within the scope of the Bancroft Library. Professor Hart's collecting zeal matched Hammond's energy; it was quite an experience to work with those two when they went into action at the same time.

In the winter of 1955–1956 I received an invitation to teach at the University of Hawaii. Neither Hammond nor John Hicks apparently, had expected that I would be willing to give up teaching permanently, and I had not succeeded in working up any sort of satisfactory part-time teaching situation while in the Bancroft. (Forty hours a week with George Hammond is full-time employment!) I remember taking my letter from Hawaii to GPH just as he finished teaching a Mexican history class in Wheeler Hall, asking if he would give me a leave of absence to try out full-time teaching. He agreed at once—and I remember his words yet: "There is nothing so grand for a scholar as having his own classroom." Later on, after I had resigned from the Library to be a full-time college teacher (or so I *thought* at the time), I remembered his words and wondered if he—the dynamic builder of the modern Bancroft Library—did not have an occasional pang for those calmer, less complicated days when his main concern could be his own lectures and his own writing.

George's regular admonition to me as his assistant was: "Let's keep the pressure on, all the way down the line." I never knew him really to let up; he might sit still and talk, but he was always keeping the pressure on. I believe that the present flourishing state of the Bancroft Library is a direct result of the superhuman energies of George P. Hammond. His successor will find that GPH's act is a hard one to follow.

A Thorough Bibliophile

Warren R. Howell

A man who loves books for themselves, who enjoys reading and own-
ing or merely holding them in his hands, who consistently expresses
himself in terms of books, is a man after my own heart. And such a
man is George P. Hammond, now for nineteen years the administrator
of one of the world's great libraries.

From the time my father founded John Howell Books in 1912, our
firm has had a relationship with the Bancroft Library more or less
close. Down through the years, he and I have known all of the Directors, personally and enjoyably, in lean times and otherwise, but the
Hammond era has been particularly satisfying. I do not speak merely
of the opportunities that have offered for us to function as I think
antiquarian bookmen should; the world has been richer for me, knowing GPH as a fellow-member of various literary and historical groups
and, ultimately, as a personal friend.

This association began almost at once after GPH assumed the directorship in July, 1946. I was immediately impressed by his imagina-
iton, his scholarship, his enterprise, his enthusiasm, and his ability to
attract people and make himself beloved by men and women of the
book world. And beyond that, to make them realize, and act upon the
realization, that they had a common interest in the welfare of the
Bancroft Library. I was honored to be one of the small group in attend-
ance at the birth of the Friends of the Bancroft Library, just a month
after GPH became Director, and like so many others I have been

47

pleased to labor, in and out of this organization, in behalf of the Library, the property of the people of the State of California, but also a national—indeed an international—treasure.

Let me show you George in action. Since 1932 my father had been trying to sell a 25-volume transcript of the minutes of the San Francisco Boards of Aldermen and Assistant Aldermen, 1852–1855. These had been copied about 1869 for "Honest Harry" Meiggs, and when the originals went up in smoke in the great fire of 1906, they were the sole reflection of the lost originals, a reflection full and faithful. They had been sold by Meiggs' heirs in 1913, finally passing into the possession of a Peruvian owner. I was very much impressed with this collection, on which a price of $10,000 had been placed. That these records should be preserved in a suitable institution was obvious, and we tried to impress others with our conviction. The effort was unavailing till GPH came along. He was convinced that Bancroft must find means to acquire these volumes, analogous as they were to H. H. Bancroft's transcripts of the destroyed records of the U.S. Surveyor General's Office, the "Archives of California." His small budget gave him no leeway to negotiate the purchase, but with characteristic imagination, GPH found a way around the road-block: Bancroft had duplicate printed works that he could undertake to trade for the manuscripts. Thus we were enabled to close the deal, paying the owner in cash. I would add that this gentleman accepted a great deal less than $10,000, because the manuscripts were going to the Bancroft Library.

Another example: In the late summer of 1947 announcement was made that the late Herbert S. Auerbach's collection of Mormon and Western books was to be auctioned in New York. If the Bancroft Library had bid in any great book auction prior to that time, I cannot name the occasion. It was always taken for granted that Bancroft had no money. Since GPH had barely begun to make headway in obtaining a regularly allocated book budget, of course he had no funds for improving upon the opportunity to fill some of the serious gaps that time had revealed in the Bancroft collections. In this instance, GPH took his case to the highest authorities of the University. He can be a persuasive man; and he got a special appropriation, relatively modest but still amounting to an unprecedented $5,000, that put Bancroft in business. It was gratifying to me that GPH saw fit to name me the Library's agent, with authority to bid at my discretion. It was also something of a challenge, to spread the available amount to maximum advantage over the three days of the sale. As I recall, I had $175 left over when the hammer fell on the last lot. A good many books came back with me from New York, among others the *Book of Mormon* (first edition, Palmyra, 1830, with the extremely rare four pages of Index). The $170 price may have seemed high to Bancroft's director, but he did not complain. Neither has he exulted that a similar copy sold in the Peter Decker sale of 1963 for $775. As a man who has himself written and published books that have become widely sought collector's items, he understands from the inside the rare book market and the forces that operate within it, the causes and the effects.

A particular reason for bringing the Friends into existence was that the organization could be a source of funds when unexpected, never recurring opportunities arose for an exciting purchase. This kind of thing, by the nature of public institutions, cannot be budgeted for. Unless and until Bancroft shall be richly endowed by its well-wishers —and that day is not yet—Bancroft requires help from a source able to act with speed and decision. The Friends began modestly, using the annual contributions of members to purchase such rarities as the available means permitted—some of these real rarities, priced accordingly, like the Mormon *Book of Commandments*; or Maximilian's *Reise in das Innere Nord-America in den Jahren 1832 bis 1834,* with the great Bodmer atlas; and this snapping up of individual items continues down to the present time. But as the Friends grew in size and strength GPH led them into more adventurous paths.

In 1955 he heard of a group of Portolá documents in Spain, offered for sale at a price of $2,000. The papers were said to deal with Portolá's first trek up the California coast from San Diego, in search of Monterey Bay. A thorough check of Bancroft's holdings having failed to turn up a single original signature by this first governor of Spanish California, GPH wrote once, and then again, to the owners in Spain, seeking more information. He succeeded in getting a vague description of the papers, but he also succeeded in upping the price to $5,000. Undeterred, GPH made arrangements for the papers to be appraised in Spain by one of the Friends. When negotiations broke down, he wrote in his courtly Spanish, asking that the papers be sent directly to him, on his faith as a reliable officer of a responsible institution that the documents would be properly looked after. The papers came on from Spain, and after a campaign to raise the purchase price, the Friends bought them for the Library in 1957. They are in the Library today because of GPH's knowledge, reputation, patience, and persistence; and because a Friends' organization existed to back him up.

This story brings another one to mind. In 1959, with my colleague Jake Zeitlin, I had the opportunity to go through the library of Martin Carrencedo in Mexico City. Carrencedo was a great accumulator of Spanish and Mexican books and manuscripts. Zeitlin and I purchased and brought back to the United States his entire collection of documents on California and the Spanish Southwest. As soon as GPH saw the collection, his imagination caught fire. No one understood better the value of this type of original source material, and the additional prestige that would come to the Bancroft Library through the acquisition of the Carrencedo collection. Consider, please, the six prime elements of this group of manuscripts:

1) Those dealing with the founding and early history of California, chiefly exemplified by three journals of Captain Rivera y Moncada, governor of Alta California from 1774–1776, which contain his correspondence with Father Junípero Serra, including eight previously unknown Serra letters.

2) Letters by Father Eusebio Kino pertaining to the beginnings of Spanish settlement in the Arizona-Sonora area.

3) An account of the exploration of the northern part of Lower California and the founding of the last of the Jesuit missions, chronicled in the diary of Father Wenceslaus Link.

4) A document telling of the settlement of San Antonio by Canary Islanders, the first civilians to reinforce the Spanish soldiery in Texas.

5) Papers relating to frontier troubles on the Texas-Rio Grande

A GPH *Portfolio*

HAMMOND ACQUISITIONS IN THE
BANCROFT LIBRARY

LIBRA
ASTRONOMICA,
Y PHILOSOPHICA
EN QUE

D. Carlos de Siguenza y Gongora
Cofmographo, y Mathematico Regio en la
Academia Mexicana,

EXAMINA
no folo lo que à fu Manifiesto Philosophico
contra los Cometas opufo

el R. P. EUSEBIO FRANCISCO KINO de la Compañia de
Jesus; fino lo que el mifmo R. P. opinò, y pretendio haver
demoftrado en fu Exposicion Astronomica
del Cometa del año de 1 6 8 1.

Sacala à luz D. SEBASTIAN DE GVZMAN Y CORDOVA,
Fator, Veedor, Provecdor, Iuez Oficial de la Real Hazienda
de fu Mageftad en la Caxa deſta Corte.

En Mexico: por los Herederos de la Viuda de BernardoCal deron
IXI. DC. XC.

PLAN. GEOGRAFO HIS-

TORICO DEL NUEUO DESCUBRI-

miento de el Puerto de Monte Rey, S.ⁿ Francifco, y las tier-
ras que fe marcaron en el derrotero de el Teniente Coro-
nel de Caballeria D.ⁿ Juan Bautifta de Anfa, Co-
mandante de la expedicion de conducion de
familias para el eftablecimiento de di-
chos Puertos.

HECHO

POR EL R. P. F. PEDRO FONT,

y facado à la letra de orden de D.ⁿ Jofé Martinez Moreno Teniente General de egidor, y Alguacil Mayor
de la Cuidad de
Queretaro.

POR

AUSENCIA DEL SEÑOR CON-

de de Regla.

Caballero del Orden  de Calatraba

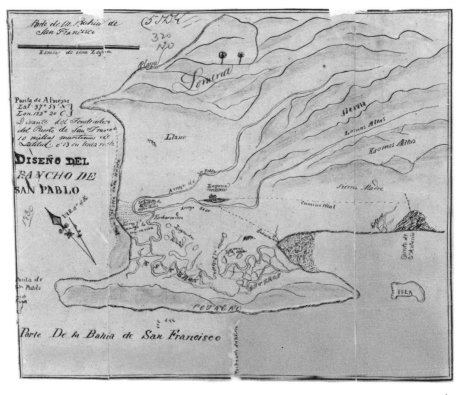

Parte de la Bahía de San Francisco

Escala de una Legua

Punta de Almejas
Lat. 37° 58' N
Lon. 122° 20' O
Distante del Fondeadero
del Puerto de San Franco
10 millas marítimas de
Latitud, o 13 en línea recta.

DISEÑO DEL
RANCHO DE
SAN PABLO

VAR. 15° 45'

Punta de
San Pablo

Sonoma

Playa

Llano

Sierra

Lomas Altas

Lomas Altas

Sierra Madre

Camino Real

Arroyo de S. Pablo

Laguna

Arroyo Seco

ISLA

POTRERO

Ensenada de S. Antonio

Parte De la Bahía de San Francisco

4

6

7

1. The Eliza Ship for California.
2. Arrival at S.ᶠ. A Monte Bank.
3. Travelling about the Mines.
4. Camping Out
5.
6. Washing Gold in a Cradle.
7. One of the few that return.
8. The End of the Many.

A View of The

Miners preparing their Fodder.

Published and Sold by Cooke & Lecount, San Francisco.

8

9

George P Hammond 1940

Peter Van Valkenburgh
1950

George P Hammond

II

border, 1797–1806, involving American invaders, Indian hostilities, and Mexican reprisals.

6) Franciscan mission reports from New Mexico and northern Mexico.

GPH urged upon the Friends the purchase of this extraordinarily rich and varied body of manuscripts, and Zeitlin and I cooperated to the limit of our ability. The Friends went to work and secured the funds necessary to bring the manuscripts to Bancroft, and they will remain there as one of the glories of the institution, a development in which Jake and I share GPH's intense satisfaction. This is the type of transaction a bookman most enjoys; and it is only possible in the environment that men like George Hammond create.

At first hand I have seen GPH working on other projects, some of them at first glance so large as to stagger onlookers—the Terrazas Collection for example; and, still more recently, the acquisition of the Robert B. Honeyman Collection of early Californian and Western American pictorial material. Susanna Dakin on a later page gives this collection its due, so I will not describe it here. This particular collection was my special pride and joy, for I had worked closely with Mr. Honeyman over a long period, bringing it together. When he decided to sell, Mr. Honeyman asked me to act as his agent. That put me in an interesting position when GPH, having heard about the pending sale, came and asked if Bancroft could buy it, for of course I was also a member of the Council of the Friends. Nevertheless, I was able to arrange matters to the satisfaction of all concerned. Mr. Honeyman was agreeable, and GPH got the Friends to work on the project of raising the impressive sum involved. He also, I would like to emphasize, gave himself wholly to the project, lecturing on the collection, addressing cogent letters to individuals and foundations, persuading, always enlightening, and finally carrying off what he rightfully regarded as a major triumph. A triumph not for himself but for the Bancroft Library.

In such labors as these we see GPH in something more than lifesize, but he reduces in his living room or yours as a man of great personal charm, alive to the smallest nuances of human relationships. For two

years, as Master of the Press, he presided with wit and learning over
the monthly meetings of the Roxburghe Club of San Francisco, occasionally speaking himself. I shall not soon forget his discourse of November 4, 1946, on "Printing and Four Centuries of New Mexican
History," when among others he paid tribute to his "hero," Don
Juan de Oñate. I have seen him leave a similar impression at sessions
of the Book Club of California, or committee meetings and special
occasions of the California Historical Society. He makes friends wherever he goes. On a trip to Spain in 1962, when he was on sabbatical
leave, I was just too late to cross his path on those far shores. The
edge was taken off my disappointment in the space of two days by an
unusually cordial welcome received from scholarly individuals happy
to greet an old friend of GPH.

Like so many busy men, and however unexplainably, George can
find time for the professional as well as the personal problems of his
friends. Sometimes real perplexities arise for a bookman, and then it
is that we thank God for the George P. Hammonds of this world.
Some years ago one of our customers was offered a collection of original documents, held in Madrid at a price of $700,000. The collection
as described included not only 16,000 pages of manuscripts relating
to Colombia, Venezuela, and Haiti between 1593 and 1870, but also
18 documents literally exciting beyond belief. These included a letter
signed and rubricated by Ferdinand and Isabella, dated 1500; a letter
written by Cortez to Emperor Charles V, dated Vera Cruz, July 10,
1519; two letters signed by Francisco Pizarro, dated Cuzco, June 10
and July 10, 1535; a watercolor map by Columbus with charts of Cuba
and Hispaniola, as well as one with the names of all the sailors on his
first voyage and paintings of the *Niña,* the *Pinta,* and the *Santa María,*
and on top of everything else, a manuscript diary of Columbus. It
seemed very probable that the 16,000 pages of manuscripts were au-
thentic, but the very splendor of those additional 18 manuscripts gave
me misgivings. I turned to GPH for counsel, and on the basis of his
report, advised my customer not to proceed with negotiations. Later
on, one of my colleagues saw this collection in Spain and reached the
conclusion that none of the documents was original. Scholars will join
me and GPH in saying: Alas!

With a man of so many diversities, it is easy to keep straying down interesting bypaths, and I want to bring these remarks back to the note on which I began, that whatever else he may be, GPH is first and last a man who loves books. He owns them in quantity—I doubt if he himself knows just how many books he owns, for he has extensive bookcases full in his home, in his Bancroft office, in his Dwinelle Hall office, in the homes of his children, no doubt, and in how many other places I could not guess. Over the years he has reviewed a large number of books, listed by Francis Farquhar on another page, and that he still has every one of those books we can rest assured. He buys beautiful new books as they are published, and beautiful old books wherever they come to his attention. Some acquired on occasional visits to Mexico he has had rebound in the entrancing style of the craftsmen there. I cannot imagine a happy GPH separated from books.

It is not surprising that such a man has literally sowed books everywhere he has been. Early in life, he had the experience shared by so many young authors, no one willing to publish the kind of books he wanted to write. It is one of the lamentable facts of life, that everyone wants to publish the books of a man who has established himself, but few show an interest in helping the man establish himself in the first place. Things are a bit different nowadays, in part because of the pioneer efforts of George Hammond, Henry R. Wagner, Herbert E. Bolton, and others, arousing interest in the Spanish era of American history, though I would not have anyone suppose that the millennium has begun. But George, and his faithful colleague Agapito Rey, believed so intensely in the value of such a document as *Obregón's History* as to adopt the costly expedient of publishing it themselves. That undertaking was a small disaster, as set forth elsewhere in this book; in another sense it was a major triumph. Out of it came the glorious Quivira series, the Coronado series, the impressive stream of publications since GPH came to the Bancroft Library.

Almost without exception, every one of these books is a thing of beauty, viewed simply as a job of bookmaking. GPH came to have a broad understanding and a deep appreciation of the niceties of book manufacturing, choice of type and paper, quality of typesetting, page make-up, binding and design. The Quivira Society volumes were already far advanced as a series when he came to the University of New Mexico in 1935. Not unnaturally, the president expressed the hope that future volumes could issue from the University Press. There might have been some delicacy about the situation, but George knew that Zimmerman was a man of reasonable and temperate mind, responsive to the facts. Patiently he pointed out the defects of the worn and broken type then being used by the Press, comparing it with the impeccable impression struck off by the plant in Pennsylvania that had been doing the Quivira printing. Zimmerman saw the light. He also found means to rectify the grievous inadequacies of the equipment at Albuquerque, and the outcome was a New Mexico University Press worth of the name—and of George P. Hammond.

This incident is by no means an isolated one. The *Guide to the Manuscript Collections of the Bancroft Library*, published as recently as 1963, might well have been mimeographed, if some counsels had prevailed. With his sense of personal and institutional style, his sense of what was *fitting*, what the very image of the Bancroft Library required, GPH stayed with the project till a fine book resulted. There will be more in the same pattern, long after he has retired. This was simply one of many unsung jobs of pioneering George has done.

"His Mild and Magnificent Eye"

SUSANNA BRYANT DAKIN

To divert his thoughts from administrative worries, Dr. Hammond often has dipped into the pictorial treasures now abounding at Bancroft. A rich variety of oil paintings, watercolors, and rare prints chosen from historical art collections acquired during the years of GPH's directorship has enlivened the drab walls of his office. From time to time there are changes in the décor, even in the site of the Director's Office. But I have noticed, as frequent visitor and amateur sleuth, that since they came into the Bancroft Library for safekeeping along with the rest of the wonderful Honeyman Collection of Early Pictorial Western Americana, certain paintings never seem to go back to the stacks. The most cursory description of some favorite works of art will reveal that GPH is a Romantic, however scholarly this tall spare man may seem on the surface:

1. "The Captive," by an unknown Romantic artist, oil painting circa 1850 [see illustration], shows a limp white woman being spirited away by a be-feathered brave riding a stallion with flowing mane and tail and flashing eyes. They are halted in flight by a translucent river. The red man looks uneasily over his shoulder at flames in the far background, but his captive seems to have forgotten her burning home. Held close to a manly chest, her eyes are closed. In bliss, or terror? This is the perennial question. Versions of "The Captive," with provocative differences, have been reproduced and discussed in

Life Magazine and *American Heritage*, and also in art historical works, as prime examples of narrative painting in the Old West.

2. "The Elopement" is a small oil by Charles Christian Nahl, acknowledged dean of resident early California painters. A dominant horse is frightening a duck and a goose off the dusty road as he gallops away with two young *Californios*. The man in sombrero and best embroidered suit holds the girl in front of him, on his silver-trimmed saddle. All in white ruffles is she, resolved to be his bride come hell or high water. A yellow, gold-threaded rebozo covers most of her hair and shoulders, harmonizing with the red-gold horse.

3. Ramona and Alessandro, heroine and hero of the best-known novel of California's Romantic period of writing and painting, may well be the lovers in a third oil—a moonlit wilderness scene called "Indian Campfire," by Charles Wimar. Tropical verdure, shining under a full moon, is depicted with consummate skill. The human figures, Rousseau-like in concept, bear little resemblance to Indians you and I have known. Like the other GPH favorites, this valuable Wimar is of modest size.

Containing all three masterpieces in their field, plus about two thousand other items varied in media, subject and value, the Honeyman is the most recent and by far the most important of all the pictorial-historical collections acquired for the Bancroft Library in the past century, through the efforts of its several Directors. Others accepted pictures, including photographs, as secondary always to manuscript, printed or microfilm material, but Dr. Hammond has sought them as valuable in themselves. He seems to have sensed that the United States was entering an intensely *visual* era at about the time he took office. Television still was in the experimental stage; such glossy magazines as *American Heritage*, *American West*, and *Horizon* were unthought-of with color processing still so expensive; even *Life* and *Look* were in the first decade of spectacular careers as ground-breakers in pictorial journalism using twentieth century reproducing techniques.

While the Past has long been the province of GPH, as historian and history professor, he has inner antennae that continually, sensitively explore the Present. This has been demonstrated time and again by his efforts on behalf of the Bancroft Library since becoming Director in the '40's. For instance, the Terrazas Collection of Mexican Revolutionary Materials was purchased with funds raised by the Friends after long, diplomatic negotiation with the Terrazas family by GPH. He was first to see that this is true source material, of un-predictable significance when used by a historian trying to understand and explain the revolutionary era through which the whole world is passing in the '60's. He beat the University of Texas to the goal post! And this is not the only time.

The *tons* of purely pictorial matter acquired through Dr. Hammond's unflagging interest and zeal (aided always by loyal staff and faithful Friends) have become a veritable mine of information and illustration, continually being worked by history students, scholars, journalists, TV and motion-picture script writers, and others of the writing fraternity. Continuous, changing exhibitions arranged by different members of the staff in the cases and on the walls of the Bancroft reading room, are of absorbing interest to school children and other daily visitors.

Over the years, about a quarter of a million historical-pictorial items have been absorbed into the Bancroft Library, a large proportion of them attracted by GPH, with his unfailing courtesy and appreciation toward even the smallest donor. Since joining the Bancroft staff in June, 1950, as head of the Public Services division, Dr. John Barr Tompkins has taken a personal interest in indexing pictorial materials and, almost as a one-man effort, he has listed no less than 43,979 paintings, drawings, prints, and photographs during moments he could spare from administrative and desk duties. That is an accomplishment for which we owe Dr. Tompkins an everlasting debt of gratitude.

The acquisition of the Honeyman Collection presented large new problems. As early as mid-1964, while funds were still being solicited by a committee intent on purchase of the Collection, GPH recognized that a new staff position must be created, to save this treasure trove from burial in the stacks, insure proper care, and assure efficient service to "haunters of the Bancroft" in years to come. Hearteningly, his plea for a qualified Curator of Pictorial Western Americana was heard and answered by the University authorities. His first choice for the position, Dr. Joseph Armstrong Baird, Jr., descended into the Bancroft underworld in the fall of 1964 and is hard at work on a catalogue of the unduplicable items collected by Robert B. Honeyman, Jr., through the expenditure of vast sums over a period of thirty-five years.

The usefulness of the many pictorial collections will be increased immeasurably by meticulous cataloguing. Accessibility is imminent for all the material indicated below (some of it virtually buried, not listed even at the time of accession):

A gift to the University of California in 1879 by the artist's widow is the spectacular Andrew Jackson Grayson Collection containing folio-sized watercolors of California and Mexican birds, painted by the 1846 pioneer to accompany his descriptive notes on western birds. Also given were sketches of scenes visited by Grayson during his natural history explorations of the West, 1853–1869. Later transferred to Bancroft, this magnificent pictorial archive was all but forgotten until the 1940's. Now, with other Grayson materials, it is being transformed into an illustrated Grayson biography by Lois Chambers Stone. Publication is imminent. Gentle prodding by GPH encouraged Mrs. Stone in an extended, often arduous undertaking.

The William A. Dougal Collection of sketches and drawings of the Californian and Central American scene, 1849–1850.

The whaling sketches, watercolor and pencil, of Captain Charles Scammon made on the spot—notably at "Scammon's Lagoon" on the Pacific Coast of Baja California—in the 1850's. This was a hidden whale calving nursery in warm, shallow waters discovered by the Maine sea captain and kept secret as long as possible. We find extraordinary contrast between his sketching and whaling moods, when comparing his pictures with entries in the log books included in the Scammon Collection. The manner of its acquisition is among the absorbing tales that GPH can tell.

Sketches by Caroline Le Conte and photographs taken by members of the famous Le Conte family on early camping trips in Yosemite Valley. Much of the Yosemite pictorial material came to the Bancroft through the courtesy of the Sierra Club. Miss Caroline's father, Professor Joseph Le Conte, was a founder of the Sierra Club, as well as the University of California.

The Peter Van Valkenburgh Collection of portraits in charcoal and pencil of prominent Californians, including GPH.

The Reuben Lucius Goldberg Collection containing no less than 5,826 original cartoons by the distinguished University of California alumnus, Class of 1904, who was awarded a Pulitzer Prize for his 1947 cartoon titled "Peace Today." Besides the cartoons, this extraordinary collection (accepted by George P. Hammond from the octogenarian himself in 1964) includes Goldberg books and articles; stills from the movie he scripted, "Soup to Nuts"; a film of "Person to Person," TV show featuring the engineer-musician-cartoonist; albums of records of radio interviews and songs with Goldberg lyrics; albums crammed with photos, clippings and letters to their friend "Rube" from such diverse persons as Adlai Stevenson, Al Capp, Bernard Baruch, Walter Winchell, Walt Disney, and Harry Truman.

A smaller cartoon collection was given by the widow of Jimmie Hatlo, who died untimely in 1963. It includes cartoon originals; proofs of his two principal series from 1942—"They'll Do It Every Time" and "Little Iodine"; and letters suggesting contemporary "foibles for his gently cauterizing attention."

The Robert B. Honeyman, Jr., Collection of Early Californian and Western Pictorial Material comprising oils, watercolors, drawings, lithographs, engravings, etchings, woodcuts, early photographs; one of the finest selections of "letter sheets" (the pictorial stationery in use by "Forty-niners" far from home, an often elegant forerunner of the common postcard) and a miscellany which includes manuscripts, maps, scrapbooks, nostalgic sheet music, childrens' games, colorful advertising cards and illustrated stock certificates issued by pioneer business concerns during the last half of the nineteenth century. Outstanding historically are the earliest surviving drawings by Spanish artists of the Malaspina round-the-world expedition that arrived in Alta California in 1791; and a watercolor dating back to the first Vancouver visit to the California coast, 1792, during a similar British expedition in the Age of Exploration. Several naturalists' notebooks are of special interest, containing notes and sketches (many in color) of wildlife fantastically varied and abundant in the late eighteenth and early nineteenth centuries; also botanical and marine-life sketches.

The Alaska Collection, mainly glass negatives of the Alaska frontier in the years 1898–1908.

The Zelda Mackay Collection of daguerreotypes, ambrotypes, and other early forms of photography.

W. H. Jackson's photographs of Alta California Missions and scenes of the Southwest.

John K. Hillers' masterful photographs of Southwestern Indians and their country.

The Jedediah Smith family portrait albums, collected in connection with Dale Morgan's productive researches on the great fur trader and explorer.

The M. M. Haseltine Collection of stereoscopic views of the West.

Timothy H. O'Sullivan's choice photographs enlarged from his negatives recording the U. S. War Department's Fortieth Parallel Survey.

The Roland Letts Oliver Collection of photographs of the Californias, Mexico and South America, viewing sailing, mining, industry, and the University of California in early days—soon after the Civil War.

Frank Schwabacher's photographs taken during the San Francisco earthquake and fire; and while camping in Yosemite Valley about the same time.

The Eadweard Muybridge Collection of photographic negatives of hundreds of stereopticon views of the West Coast from Alaska to Yosemite, made from the originals owned by the San Francisco College for Women and obtained through the courtesy of the Reverend Mother Mejia and Mother Cassidy.

Mason Weymouth's photographs of "The Changing Scene" in San Francisco.

From the Historic American Buildings Survey, a selection of photographs of historic buildings of California and Nevada (from the files of the National Park Service, San Francisco Office).

Edwin M. Blake's own photographs of the West, notably the western National Parks.

Howard Willoughby's collection of photographs of the Old West.

Wyland Stanley's Iconography of San Francisco, mainly, and of Oakland.

The Moses Cohen Collection of Oakland press and commercial photographs of the Bay Area.

More than *two tons* of material from the picture file of the *San Francisco Call* daily newspaper, 1916–1950. And so on. . . .

The sheer weight of the *Call* gift crushes my spirit. I find it more appealing to riffle through collections not purely pictorial, like those of the Le Conte family and Captain Scammon. Here, one happens upon an engaging journal written and illustrated by a fourteen-year-old girl, camping luxuriously with a family party and a Chinese cook in "Yo Semite" in 1878; there, upon a watercolor sketch done with surprising sensitivity by a hardened whaler observing a mother at play with her large baby in a tropical lagoon.

Although intriguing, it is wasteful of time and intelligence for too much to be left to chance discovery. Only when cataloguing is further advanced can full use be made of the treasure trove amassed mostly through the gentle, yet firm prodding of GPH. Frequenters of such an institution as Bancroft often need guidance, especially when engaged in the unending, un-predictable process of research. We welcome Dr. Baird's appointment as an important step forward in public service—planned, of course, by GPH.

When George Hammond retires this year, where will his like be found? He seems to have lived in spirit with the painters whose work he so deeply admires. As the "Old Master" William Keith said of these Romantics: "The country was young then, and men could see the poetry and romance . . . that lay at their own doors." Hammond doors have been opened for me, through the years. With so many others of all ages and varied interests, I have been allowed to share the vision of a rare, unassuming man. As in "The Lost Leader" (Browning's tribute to Wordsworth), it can be truly said that we

> ". . . followed him, honored him,
> Lived in his mild and magnificent eye."

Remarks on the Occasion of the Wagner Award

J. S. HOLLIDAY

Recently a friend called my attention to a passage in Walt Whitman's *Leaves of Grass*, wherein the poet inquires: "Who are you indeed who would talk or sing to America?" Whitman then poses a series of questions—questions which bring to my mind George P. Hammond:

> "Have you studied out the land, its idioms and men?
> Have you learned the physiology, phrenology, politics, geography, pride, freedom, friendship of the land?
> Have you sped through fleeting customs, popularities?
> Can you hold your hand against all follies, whirls, fierce contentions?
> Are you very strong?
> Have you, too, the old, ever-fresh forbearance and impartiality?"

To know George Hammond, scholar and man, is to find positive answers to these searching questions—how carefully, thoughtfully he has studied the great West, its geography, its men, its prides and friendships, past and present—what whirls and fierce contentions he has weathered by maintaining his calm forbearance and impartiality —what strength of purpose and of integrity he has exhibited through the years.

I speak of these qualities of the man because the scholar and the man cannot be separated, especially not on this occasion. The Henry R. Wagner Memorial Award in a few years has achieved its value and recognition not alone for the scholarship it has honored but as well for the quality of the men—men of strength and fineness: Carl I. Wheat, Rev. Maynard Geiger, Dale L. Morgan, Thomas W. Streeter. To-night's recipient joins these, his predecessors, as a man and a scholar who both enhances and deserves this award.

Quickly—for there are only a few minutes—I will speak of George Hammond: the scholar-author, the scholar-administrator, and of the man himself.

The award being given tonight cites Hammond's "compilation, annotation, and scholarly editing of the comprehensive edition of *The Larkin Papers—Personal, Business and Official Correspondence of Thomas Oliver Larkin, Merchant and United States Consul in California.*" Published by the University of California Press in ten volumes (the tenth came out this year), they total some 3,500 pages of many hundreds of documents, each meticulously transcribed from the handwritten original, selected from the Bancroft Library's Larkin Collection of over 4,000 letters to Larkin and copies of his official correspondence to the Secretaries of State and Navy—covering the period from 1822 to Larkin's death in 1858. These ten volumes are a monumental achievement, made possible by Hammond's unique combination of talents: an unrelenting purposefulness, an extensive experience as an editor of basic historic documents, and an intimate knowledge of early California history. Nothing less could have done the job.

To refresh my knowledge and appreciation of *The Larkin Papers*, I read through consecutively the ten introductions written by Hammond over a span of thirteen years. (The first volume was published in 1951.) These introductions reveal—indeed, they emphasize—the special qualities of George Hammond the scholar: his careful orderliness midst a complexity and diversity of events and people; his 360° awareness; and his never-failing ability to convey the mood, the color, the realities of the past. To draw the essentials from 4,000 letters and records of business affairs and official reports; to order them and retain always the flavor and mood of the times and of the people; to express lucidly, forthrightly the historian's judgment of events and their causes—to do all this is the work of a master historian and editor, and that is the work exhibited in the ten introductions which open the way to the richness of the documents themselves.

And what of these Larkin papers? I can do no better than to quote George Hammond's assessment of their value, written when he first began the task of preparing them for publication: "Such original sources are never exhausted, no matter how often they are used. To one writer they serve one purpose—to another, still another. So it is that today these famous old manuscripts are being consulted by new generations. To them the records, old and hoary with tradition, are truly new discoveries. Indeed, that is how it will be a hundred or five hundred years from now. It is therefore our responsibility to make sure that they last that long." With the publication of Volume Ten, that responsibility has been fulfilled.

I cannot resist quoting a few lines from *The Larkin Papers*, lines that will tell you something of the value and appeal of these letters and of the Hammond introductions. For instance, Larkin speaking of matrimony: "All love and no capital will never do for me." And Larkin writing in San Francisco during the height of the gold rush turmoil: "My head whirls with speculation; my hair grows gray by excessive working of my brain and ambition." And Jacob Leese, writing to his friend Larkin in 1850, when Larkin was thinking of taking up residence in New York: "Here you wil be a lyon and there you wil hav to be as cunning as a fox."

These and scores of other rich and memorable quotes are woven into the introductions. And there are descriptive scenes by Hammond. For instance, a social event in April, 1846: The *Portsmouth* has anchored at Monterey, and the chief Mexican and California families invite Captain Montgomery and his officers to a picnic in the country. Hammond writes: "When the day came, a large part of the population gathered at the American consulate. . . . In small groups they rode the twelve or fourteen miles to the pleasure grounds. All the officers who could leave the ship went along. . . . It must have been a sprightly sight to see the whole party, a hundred strong or more, riding past Carmel Mission at a trot or gallop, some of the women riding double (the woman in the saddle, the man behind) and a file of soldiers out in front with banners flying from the tips of their lances." *There* is a scene to give substance to our visions of Pastoral California!

All this and so much more is found in these hundred pages of introductions, which are in effect a distillation of the thousands of Larkin documents, a brilliant summary of the economic, political, and human forces that shaped California history during the 1830's, '40's, and '50's.

The Larkin Papers, though ten volumes and thirteen years' work, are but one title in a bibliography of Hammond's publications. A recent count totaled eighty-seven titles, excluding book reviews. These evidences of scholarship and of perseverance are but one dimension of George Hammond's scholarly career. Since coming to the University of California at Berkeley in 1946, he has been a member of the History Department, lending to it a steadying influence and a prestigious reputation. And through the years he has carried on his teaching, with lecture courses for undergraduates and seminars for graduate students.

Beyond this, there are the eighteen years of his directorship of the Bancroft Library, years that have added new lustre and significance to the tradition of scholarly leadership for the library. That tradition began with Hubert Howe Bancroft in the 1860's, continued through the years of Herbert Bolton. The Hammond years commenced in 1946 and have been marked by the constant expansion and deep enrichment of Bancroft's resources. Already a scholar of note when he came to the library, Hammond has never allowed his research and writing to deflect him from the great task of building Bancroft Library. And what a builder he has been!

I will mention only a few of the foundation stones that Hammond has put into place to support the recent and the future growth of the library—The Friends of the Bancroft Library: they have been the cornerstone of the Hammond administration, and they are a tribute to his faith in his Friends and their faith in him—The great Terrazas Collection, which was acquired by the main force of Hammond's confidence that this collection would serve the University for years to come as a major source for the study of the Mexican Revolution. It was that confidence, so quiet, but so persuasive, that brought about the decisions needed to raise the funds. The same was true of the recently purchased Honeyman Collection: undismayed by the half-million dollar price, convinced of the long-term value, Hammond and his Friends set about persuading and enlightening—and now that unexcelled visual record of California and the West is part of the vast pictorial collection of the Bancroft Library.

And another asset of the Library: Dale L. Morgan, brought to the staff by Hammond in 1954. What an eminence is he in Western history, and what a team Hammond & Morgan have been, as evidenced by *The Guide to the Manuscript Collections of the Bancroft Library*, the first volume of which was published in 1963; and as evidenced by their daily rapport, their mutual assistance on a dozen projects and productions for Bancroft. This scholarly alliance embraces many members of the Bancroft Library staff—men and women who under the encouragement of Hammond have also found time to produce significant articles and books on California and Western history. The list of their publications is too long to be recited tonight, but representative are Helen H. Bretnor's recent editing of E. C. Kemble's history of early California newspapers and Robert H. Becker's forthcoming *Diseños of California Ranchos. Maps of thirty-seven Land Grants [1822–1846]*, to be published by the Book Club of California: a book that will surely set a new standard of creative scholarship. These and other examples of research and writing have given the Bancroft staff a special feel, an empathy for the needs of scholars.

The Bancroft Library is today stronger than ever before: stronger in its foundations of unexcelled resources, stronger in the breadth of its reputation, stronger in its magnetic attraction to scholars around the world. These strengths are lasting tributes to George Hammond, the scholar-administrator.

Finally, the man ... a quiet man, but never still; a modest man, but never naïve; a patient man, but never satisfied. And a man who knows not how to blow his own trumpet—instead he allows his work to speak for him. And how eloquent it is. But how good it is that there are Wagner Awards, occasions such as this, which speak loudly and lastingly in recognizing the scholar and his work when both have the strength and the substance to survive fleeting customs and popularities.

Remarks on the Occasion of the Serra Award

FRANCE V. SCHOLES

Mr. Chairman, my dear friend George Peter, Reverend Fathers, Gentlemen:

Several years ago, in a speech I made here when Carlos Castañeda received the Serra Award, I said that for me an invitation of the Academy of American Franciscan History was a command. And so it was recently when Father Kieman invited me to take part in these ceremonies tonight. I welcomed this new command because it offered the opportunity once more publicly to express appreciation of the signal honors the Academy, since its foundation, has conferred upon me— and also, because of my profound admiration for the guest of honor, who has been my loyal friend for more than thirty years.

This long friendship has been characterized during its entire course by a common interest in the history of the Spanish Southwest and colonial Latin America. It was this common interest, and more specifically the history of New Mexico, which prompted our first meeting in Los Angeles in 1931, when he was on the faculty of the University of Southern California and I was on the staff of the University of New Mexico. Indeed, our respective academic careers have been conditioned in considerable measure by New Mexico and the New Mexican scene. For eleven years, 1935–1946, he served as Chairman of the History Department and as Dean of the Graduate School in the

University of New Mexico. With the exception of twelve years, 1926–1928 and 1931–1941, New Mexico has been my home since 1924, when I first arrived in Albuquerque in search of health. In 1946, when Dr. Hammond became Director of the Bancroft Library, I succeeded him as Graduate Dean at New Mexico. During all these years we have maintained professional and, at times, rather close personal contacts. He has shared with me his vast knowledge of the resources for the history of the Spanish Borderlands and colonial Mexico, and I have tried to reciprocate by sharing with him my research experiences and the findings of my own investigations. From time to time we have labored together in the pursuit of common scholarly objectives.

Surely this long and happy relationship has given me some right to assess the qualities of mind and character of the guest of honor and to evaluate the achievements of his total career. Accordingly, I wish to suggest, first of all, that the most significant feature of his career is the obvious fact that he has successfully combined teaching, administrative responsibilities, research, and publication. He has demonstrated that such activities are not necessarily incompatible—that in the final analysis, scholarly achievement reflects individual and compulsive motivations, which find expression regardless of external or deterrent conditions.

During his tenure as Chairman of the History Department and Graduate Dean at the University of New Mexico, Dr. Hammond taught undergraduate and graduate level courses with skill and enthusiasm, as attested by reports given me by many of his students. And at California also, for more than a decade he lectured to large classes, directed graduate theses and dissertations, and served as examiner for Ph.D. candidates. A member of the faculty of a New Mexico state college, who wrote his dissertation under Dr. Hammond's direction, has expressed to me admiration and affection for his mentor and master.

When Dr. Hammond became Graduate Dean at New Mexico in 1935, President Zimmerman charged him with responsibility for developing a regional program of graduate instruction that would place major emphasis on anthropology, Spanish language and literature,

Southwestern and Latin American history, geology and ethnobiology —fields in which the University, because of its location and special resources, might expect to achieve competence and distinction. Although some progress had already been made in this direction, the new dean at first faced some rather serious obstacles in carrying out this plan. There were staff problems, including inertia and opposition on the part of some of his faculty colleagues. Laboratory facilities and library holdings were deficient. The Depression of the 1930's clouded the scene. But perseverance, a kind of grim determination, and also a healthy optimism have always characterized this man, and by 1940 considerable progress had been made. Then came War and during his last years at New Mexico he must have had moments of doubt as to the permanent end results of his effort.

I do not know how he, in retrospect, views these eleven years of devoted service, with their victories and also their frustrations, but I can give you the judgment of one man, who observed his work at rather close range during part of this time and who followed in his path in the Graduate Office.

Without question, George Hammond deserves credit for the establishment on a sound basis of the regional program of research and advanced study that to this day has been a distinctive feature of the University curriculum. During those eleven years this regional program was accorded recognition in the form of generous foundation grants to augment library holdings in the fields of anthropology and Spanish and Spanish American literature and history. If the New Mexico history department today enjoys some reputation as a center for the study of Latin American history, this also may be attributed in no small measure to the orientation that he gave to departmental course offerings. In the formation of the collection of archival and other documentary sources for Western American and Hispanic American history in the University library he played a major role. His enthusiasm and zeal in this respect may be illustrated by the fact, sometimes forgotten or ignored in the University today, that he often spent days and entire weekends in the photo laboratory of the library making enlargement prints from microfilm facsimiles of documentation in Spanish and Mexican archives. And finally, during these years as teacher and administrator at New Mexico, he supervised the preparation of important volumes of the Quivira Society Publications, inaugurated in 1940 the Coronado Cuarto Centennial Series, and personally edited two volumes of this Series—the narratives of the Coronado expedition and Benavides' Revised Memorial of 1634. He has since added *Oñate, Colonizer of New Mexico,* in two fat volumes.

These New Mexico years may be regarded perhaps as a kind of testing time for his later career as Director of Bancroft Library, where he faced an even greater challenge. During the ten to twenty years prior to 1946 the Bancroft collections, because of the Depression and World War II, had not been accorded adequate financial support. The Library was serviced by a very small staff; space facilities were cramped and inadequate; university budgets made no provision for new book purchases or for the employment of specially trained manuscript cataloguers; the Library lacked funds for the acquisition of new manuscript collections. Consequently the primacy of Bancroft in the field of Western Americana was being threatened by other libraries.

Today, eighteen years later, any person who has eyes to see or ears to hear—if he will use his eyes and ears!—must agree that the picture has changed, that the Bancroft Library has been revitalized, thanks to the vision, leadership, dynamism, and driving energy of George Hammond. In past years I often observed his agile, swinging stride as he moved across the University of New Mexico campus, and I venture the suggestion that a similar resilient quality—a quality of mind and purpose—has enabled him at Berkeley to overcome obstacles which, at times, may have seemed insurmountable, to enlist support within the University and from outside sources, and to move forward with confidence toward the realization of his dream for a new and greater Bancroft dedicated to the advancement of learning and to the enrichment of the cultural heritage of California and the entire Pacific Coast community.

The measure of his success as Director of Bancroft Library may be illustrated by a recital of some of the significant developments during the past eighteen years. Annual budgets for book purchases, nonexistent in 1946, now approach $30,000. The Library staff has been increased from five or six to more than twenty, including acquisition and catalogue specialists; new methods and procedures for the cataloguing of the manuscript collections have been devised. The research resources of the Library have been augmented by the acquisition of new collections, and also by a vast store of microfilm facsimiles of documentation relating to the history of Western America and Latin America in the archives of Great Britain, France, Holland, Spain, Portugal, Mexico, and other countries. Perhaps the most significant development has been the enlistment of enthusiastic patrons, the Friends of the Bancroft Library, now more than a thousand, who have provided funds for the purchase of new manuscript collections and for the inauguration of a Bancroft Library Publications series.

In short, Bancroft's primacy among Pacific Coast libraries has been restored and assured; and, if I may employ a splashy phrase, the Bancroft Library is now one of the brightest jewels in the University of California's crown of glory!

Although Dr. Hammond's administrative services at the University of New Mexico and the University of California have been characterized by notable achievements, I feel certain that if he were asked to define that phase of his academic career from which he has derived the greatest personal satisfaction, the answer would be his scholarly research and the publication of documentary sources relating to the history of northern Mexico and the Spanish Southwest. I feel certain of this because it is what he has been doing for almost forty years. His first publication of this kind, a translation of Baltasar de Obregón's chronicle of exploration and conquest in northern Mexico in the sixteenth century, appeared in 1928. And he now has in press a new volume of documents on New Mexico exploration, 1581–1595. During the period from 1928 to 1964–65 he has edited and published at fairly regular intervals many other volumes of similar content on the history of colonial Mexico and the Spanish Borderlands.

I am sure that he would want me to mention in this connection the collaboration of Agapito Rey in the preparation of many of these publications. This Hammond and Rey scholarly partnership, formed when they were young teachers at the University of North Dakota in the 1920's, has had a potent and fruitful influence on the modern historiography of Western America.

Enumeration of the titles of Dr. Hammond's publications would be out of place here; in the presence of this company it would be a kind of impertinence, for these volumes constitute an indispensable resource for your teaching and research. Indeed, it is difficult to imagine how any college course on colonial Mexico and the Borderlands can be taught without resort to them.

But any just evaluation of his total contribution to the historiography of the Spanish Borderlands must also take account of his general editorship of the Quivira Society Publications and the Coronado Cuarto Centennial Series, of which thirteen and ten volumes respectively have appeared. Both of these series he has planned and edited while he has been engaged in teaching and university administration.

The Quivira Society Publications, of which the first volume appeared in 1929, reflect the dream and aspirations of a young scholar brought to fruition by his own efforts. Volumes of this series have contained a page listing members of a Quivira Society Council. My name appears on this list. But I know, and other Council members have known, that the Quivira Publications have been the work of one man, that the Quivira Society was George Peter Hammond. And also let me say for the record tonight, that the Quivira Publications were not subsidized by any national agency or foundation, that the editor pledged his own resources to finance them, and that more than once he paid printing bills out of his own pocket. I wonder how many young scholars today, how many members of university faculties would do the same, or feel the need to do so. This question prompts the observation that the present-day plethora of research funds being made available by foundations and governmental agencies has not been an unmixed blessing. It has resulted, I fear, in the temptation to formulate research and publication projects, not in terms of a basic and personal scholarly interest, but rather in terms of prospects for financial support. "Grantsmanship" has become an unfortunate and unsavory feature of academic life.

Recently I had access to a reader's report on an article submitted by a young scholar for publication in a professional journal. The reader criticized the article on several counts, some of which, I thought, were not just. But the most disturbing feature of the critique, in my opinion, was the statement that the article reflected failure by its author to appreciate or understand "the right questions" of modern historical research. What are these "right questions," and who should have the authority to define them? The writing of history has always been characterized, of course, by changing fashions, tastes, and emphases, and God grant that this may be true in the future. But to condemn an honest piece of research in terms of a doctrine of "right questions" smacks of arrogance and intolerance; it challenges the historian's privilege and duty to be the master of his craft, and to give expression to the compulsive and individual motivations which have been the mainsprings and inspiration of solid and distinguished historical achievement.

I doubt that George Hammond has ever been very much concerned about "the right questions" of historical research. But he has had compulsive motivations. Within his mind and heart there has been a voice saying: "This is what I want to do; this is what I must do." And in response to this voice he has followed a true and consistent course to success and distinction.

Some of you present here tonight have heard me on other occasions make reference to a famous Latin ode in which Horace affirmed that his poetry would survive the ravages of time. In the sixth verse of this ode there is the exultant phrase, "*non omnis moriar*." And so tonight, in the presence of George Hammond and this distinguished company, I wish to affirm the conviction that his work will endure and live beyond his time—that, to adapt the words of Horace, not all of him will die.

Response to the Academy
of American Franciscan History

GEORGE P. HAMMOND

For the generous words that have been voiced here this evening, and for the presentation to me of the Serra Award of the Americas for 1964, I can only say, "Thank you." I am profoundly grateful. Let me add that I feel this honor is given not only in recognition of the work I have done, but also as a tribute to the institution that I have represented for many years, the Bancroft Library of the University of California.

To France Scholes, friend and associate of a lifetime, I wish to say a special word of thanks for coming to this ceremony and for his kind remarks. Many times our paths have crossed; we have tilled the same fields of Southwestern history, but each of us has gone farther afield in pursuit of his own interests.

There is a saying that it is a privilege of the old to reminisce; without presuming too much on your patience, I should like to indulge in that pastime for a few moments.

Life for me has been an exciting adventure, like traveling through a strange country without knowing the way or what might happen. My parents gave me a rigorous upbringing, and if it is true that as the twig is bent so the tree will grow, I owe them a great debt. They humored me when I insisted on going to school. But they left little

77

place for frivolity in life; they taught me to work hard, live frugally, and walk a straight and narrow path.

Withal, life has been an exciting adventure: every path that I have trod, every detour, has had its reward. One begins his work in the teaching profession with faltering steps, perhaps, but he gains strength and confidence; and when he becomes an instructor or professor in an educational institution of higher learning, he is truly "on his own." I started that way. To me, as a young man, the University was something of a "dream world," for I had never anticipated a career in it. But my high school principal coached me for four years, and saw to it that I went to the University of California (then consisting only of a Berkeley campus), where I came under the influence of many fine teachers, among them Henry Morse Stephens, Louis John Paetow, and Herbert E. Bolton of the history department, and others like Monroe E. Deutsch in Latin or E. Kurt Heller in German. Bolton, you will recall, was honored with the Americas Award by this Academy in 1949.

From the first, I strove simply to do my teaching job well, but a year in the Archives of the Indies as a Native Sons of the Golden West Fellow in History, close association with the seminars given by Bolton, and intimate acquaintance with men like Henry R. Wagner and Frederick Webb Hodge, led me inevitably to nourish ambitions to publish some of my own research. As I look back, much of this could have been done better, but that is hindsight—that is part of the road that has been trod. I was young; life seemed rosy; I enjoyed tremendously the inspiration that came from my students—graduate and undergraduate; and then in 1935, I was led off into one of the detours of University life—*i.e.*, into administrative responsibility—a detour that at the time seemed flattering, but which ever after (though I did not realize it at the time) hampered the opportunity for development in the fields of teaching, research, and writing. Modern University life has become so complex, so demanding, that anyone who accepts administrative duties will find that in all probability it will impair the effectiveness of his teaching and creative work.

At New Mexico, I had eleven interesting years. Special assignments included getting the faculty to approve the granting of the Ph. D. degree in three departments—Anthropology, History, and English—as peculiarly appropriate to the Southwest; helping to build the Library, and making a beginning on what has become known as the Coronado Library; launching what became the 12-volume Coronado Historical Series; and also helping President James Fulton Zimmerman in formulating ideas for what became the Statewide Coronado Cuarto Centennial Celebration of 1940.

Bancroft, when I came there in 1946, seemed like a nice, quiet place, and it took some time for me to become oriented, to learn University administrative procedures, to develop a vision of Bancroft's part in the University of California's library structure—what it was, what it could be, and what in my judgment it ought to be. I came to feel that the Bancroft Library should strive to remain what it had been in H. H. Bancroft's day—the fountainhead of research in Western and Latin American history. But that meant growth—more staff, money for books, documents, microfilms, binding—everything. In addition to long-range plans, it meant getting some "ready money." When an opportunity for a great purchase came along, always beyond the capacity of the regular budget, one could not wait for a request to go "through channels." That meant delay—endless delay—without assurance of getting it. If the money came through, it might be too late to be of use. You know this kind of situation well!

It was my conviction that the University of California should support the Bancroft Library as the greatest treasure in its Library firmament; that this kind of support would pay handsome dividends in prestige for the University, that the numerous branch libraries (all good in themselves) would in the long run profit by keeping the Bancroft Library as the bellwether in its library system. It took a long time to get this message across, if indeed it did—I am not so sure of that. My successor will have to fight this battle with unceasing vigor.

In a sense only, these were new ideas. Actually, they were the old ideas of Hubert Howe Bancroft and Herbert Eugene Bolton. It became clear that it was not enough to exploit the resources of the Library. New resources had to be added in greater measure to keep pace with changing conditions, addition of new campuses to the University system, with the growth of University enrollment, with the mass of historical documentation that was and is accumulating in our own time.

In these various activities we have had modest success. Bancroft now has about 135,000 volumes, in addition to its great collection of maps, manuscripts, newspapers, microfilms, and historical pictures, lithographs, and similar research materials. We have established a separate department to care for and catalogue the manuscript collections, a move that I consider a real achievement. We have also set up a microfilm department, which handles all of our microfilm, from whatever source it comes, and catalogues and keeps the film in order and available.

We have also developed an active policy for collecting recent Californiana and other sources—political, social and business history. This already includes the papers of several California governors, senators, and representatives, as well as poets, writers and interpreters of modern life, other leaders of public opinion, as well as the papers of some important business firms, including forestry and lumbering, which have had an important place in California history from the earliest days.

To make the Library's holdings known, we have launched a *Guide* series of our manuscript sources; one volume has been published; others are in preparation.

Finally, the work of the Bancroft Library has been enormously strengthened by the Friends of the Bancroft Library, an organization that was formed in 1946 for the simple purpose of increasing the usefulness of the Library. Without the dedicated help of its leaders and the members whose contributions support it, it would not have been possible to do many of the things that have been done. The Friends, gathering strength slowly, helped us acquire a collection of early California documents, dating from the 1770's (cost nearly $50,000); the Silvestre Terrazas Collection relating to the Mexican Revolution of 1910 (cost $75,000); The Honeyman Collection of Western pictorial Americana (the latter at a cost of $550,000).

These are high points—red-letter days in the history of an institution. In addition, literally thousands of gifts— some of great importance, have come to us. All of these acquisitions are of significance for the scholar in Western American or Latin American history. It is my hope that these steps are but harbingers of what may be done in the future. The growth of the University of California and its many campuses makes such a program imperative. The possibilities for future growth of the Library are great, and I envy my successor the scope of the task—the challenge of what may be done. It is a tremendous responsibility—a real opportunity for public service.

A library must be a growing organism if it is to serve its purpose in modern society. It cannot deal only with the gold rush or other early events. It must deal with and collect the sources of modern life—the struggle of minorities, various individual groups of society (even the so-called Free Speech Movement which is now ravaging our campus), and other issues, capital or labor, and a thousand similar subjects. We in America are still a young nation. A hundred years from now the events of the years we are passing through may be looked on as of signal importance. Who is collecting the sources, the materials of today that will be available 25 or 50 years from now for the use of our grandchildren? In this developing program every library must play its part, including the Bancroft and probably this Academy.

I look to the future with confidence, certain that the University of California and the people of the state will support its great libraries, for without them there cannot be a great faculty, nor a great and intelligent student body. In the field of California and Western history, the Bancroft is the leader. I feel sure that the faculty and administrative leaders of the University will keep it so.

George P. Hammond's Publications

FRANCIS P. FARQUHAR

Compiled with the aid of Helen Harding Bretnor, J. S. Holliday and Dale L. Morgan

Abbreviations:

AHR	American Historical Review
CHSQ	California Historical Society Quarterly
HAHR	Hispanic American Historical Review
MVHR	Mississippi Valley Historical Review
NMHR	New Mexico Historical Review
PHR	Pacific Historical Review
PNWQ	Pacific Northwest Quarterly
SCQ	Southern California Quarterly
SWHQ	Southwestern Historical Quarterly
UHQ	Utah Historical Quarterly

Citations to periodicals are to volume and issue, with page numbers following, *e.g.*: (37: 4: 486–488).

THESES AND GENERAL PUBLICATIONS

1921 *German Interest in California Before 1850.* A. M. thesis, University of California, Berkeley, 1921. xx, 162 l. Unpublished.

1923 "Some Impressions of Spain," University of North Dakota *Quarterly Journal*, November, 1923 (14: 1: 70–81). Republished herein.

1924 *Don Juan de Oñate and the Founding of New Mexico.* Ph. D. thesis,

83

University of California, Berkeley, 1924. xii, 399 l. Published in revised and condensed form in 1926–1927; see below.

1925   "The Desertion of Oñate's Colony from New Mexico," University of North Dakota *Quarterly Journal*, January, 1925 (15: 2: 154–167).

1926–1927   "Don Juan de Oñate and the Founding of New Mexico," *NMHR*, January, 1926–April, 1927 (1: 1–4: 42–77, 156–192, 292–323, 445–477; 2: 1–2: 37–66, 134–174). Revised and condensed version of the Ph. D. thesis of 1924. Also printed separately; see next below.

1927   *Don Juan de Oñate and the Founding of New Mexico* ..., Historical Society of New Mexico Publications in History, II, Santa Fe, October, 1927. vii, 228 p. GPH's first book, reprinted after serialization (next above).

1927   GPH and Agapito Rey, "The Rodríguez Expedition to New Mexico, 1581–1582," *NMHR*, July–October, 1927 (2: 3–4: 239–268, 334–362). Also printed separately; see next below.

1927   GPH and Agapito Rey, *The Gallegos Relation of the Rodríguez Expedition to New Mexico*, Historical Society of New Mexico Publications in History, IV, Santa Fe, December, 1927. 69 p. The first-published joint book by Hammond and Rey, reprinted after serialization (next above).

1928   GPH and Agapito Rey, *Obregón's History of 16th Century Explorations In Western America, entitled Chronicle, Commentary, or Relation of the Ancient and Modern Discoveries in New Spain and Mexico, Mexico, 1584*, Los Angeles, 1928. xxiv, 351 p.

1929   GPH and Agapito Rey, *Expedition into New Mexico Made by Antonio de Espejo, 1582–1583, as Revealed in the Journal of Diego Pérez de Luxán, a Member of the Party* ..., Quivira Society Publications, I, Los Angeles, 1929, 143 p. (500 copies printed, 30 on large paper.)

1929   "Pimería Alta after Kino's Time," *NMHR*, July, 1929 (4: 3: 220–238). Documents written to Dr. Don Benito Crespo, January 7, 1737. Also printed separately.

1929   "The Camp Grant Massacre: A Chapter in Apache History,"

American Historical Association, Pacific Coast Branch, *Proceedings*, 1929–1930, p. 200–215. Also printed separately.

1931   "The [José] Zúñiga Journal, Tucson to Santa Fé: The Opening of a Spanish Trade Route, 1788–1795," *NMHR*, January, 1931 (6: 4: 40–65). Also printed separately.

1931   *History of the Pacific District of the United Danish Evangelical Lutheran Church, 1888–1930, commemorating the 25th Anniversary since the reorganization of the Pacific District on a delegate basis.* [Los Angeles, 1931. Published by the Pacific District; printed in Danish Lutheran Publishing House, Blair, Nebraska.] 55 p. Foreword is signed A. P. Juhl, Easton; George P. Hammond, Los Angeles; H. P. Hansen, Fresno; Rev. Carl Wilhelmsen, Fresno; notwithstanding, the book was assembled, revised, and edited by GPH. The work includes an account of "Our Saviour's [Church], Caruthers," with information on the N. P. J. Hammond family in that locality from 1909.

1932   "The Conviction of Don Juan de Oñate, New Mexico's First Governor," *New Spain and the Anglo-American West; Historical Contributions Presented to Herbert Eugene Bolton*, Los Angeles, 1932, 2 vols., vol. 1, pp. 69 74. For this book see under EDITORIAL.

1932   Foreword to Phil Townsend Hanna, *Mexico in the Machine Age. A Plea for Industrial Freedom*, Los Angeles, Alpha Delta Iota, 1932. 33 p. (250 copies printed.)

1935   "Oñate a Marauder?" *NMHR*, October, 1935 (10: 4: 249–270). Also printed separately.

1936   "Latin-American Attitudes toward the United States," in Southern Methodist University, Institute of Public Affairs, *3rd Conference*, Dallas, 1936, pp. 92–105.

1936   GPH and Thomas C. Donnelly, *The Story of New Mexico, Its History and Government*, Albuquerque, 1936. 331 p. A revised edition was published in 1941; see below.

1938   "Oñate's Appointment as Governor of New Mexico," *NMHR*, July, 1938 (13: 3: 241–254).

1938   GPH and Agapito Rey, *New Mexico in 1602. Juan de Montoya's*

Relation of the Discovery of New Mexico, Quivira Society Publications, VIII, Albuquerque, 1938. 143 p. (550 copies printed.)

1938   GPH and Edgar F. Goad, *The Adventure of Don Francisco Vásquez de Coronado,* Albuquerque, 1938. vi, 140 p.

1939   Foreword to Miguel Antonio Otero, *My Life on the Frontier, 1882–1897,* Albuquerque, 1939. xi, 306 p. GPH's editorial involvement in this second volume of Otero's reminiscences was more extensive than the foreword intimates. In all, the Otero reminiscences ran to three volumes: GPH had no part in the first and third.

1939   "Manuscript Collections in the Spanish Archives in New Mexico," *Archives and Libraries,* Chicago, 1939, pp. 80–87. A paper presented at "the 1939 Conference of the American Library Association representing the joint program of the Committee on Archives and Libraries of the A. L. A., the Pacific Coast Members of the Society of American Archivists and the Historical Records Survey." Planographed.

1939   *The Quivira Society, a Decade of Progress, 1929–1939* [Albuquerque, 1939]. 15 p. Unsigned introduction by GPH to a catalogue of the Society's first ten titles.

1940   Foreword to Leslie A. White, *Pioneers in American Anthropology; The Bandelier-Morgan Letters,* Albuquerque, 1940. 2 vols., [xv] 272; [vi], 266 p. See under EDITORIAL.

1940   *Coronado's Seven Cities,* Albuquerque, United States Coronado Exposition Commission, 1940. iv, 82 p.

1940   "Francisco Vasquez de Coronado, Conquistador," Minnequa Historical Society [of Pueblo, Colorado], *Bulletin,* Spring, 1940 (23–29). Mimeographed.

1940   GPH and Agapito Rey, *Narratives of the Coronado Expedition, 1540–1542,* Coronado Cuarto Centennial Publications, II, Albuquerque, 1940. xii, 413 p.

1941   GPH and Thomas C. Donnelly, *The Story of New Mexico, Its History and Government,* Albuquerque, 1941. 333 p. Revised edition of the book published in 1936.

1945   "Argentina in Turmoil," *The Historian,* Autumn, 1945 (8: 1: 46–61).

1945 GPH, Frederick Webb Hodge, and Agapito Rey, *Fray Alonso de Benavides' Revised Memorial of 1634*, Coronado Cuarto Centennial Publications, IV, Albuquerque, 1945. xvi, 368 p.

1946 Introduction to *The Discovery of Florida, being a true relation of the vicissitudes that attended the governor Don Hernando de Soto and some nobles of Portugal in the discovery of Florida, now just given by a fidalgo of Elvas. Translated by Buckingham Smith*, San Francisco, printed at the Grabhorn Press for the Book Club of California, 1946. vi, 105 p. (280 copies printed.)

1948 "Sutter to Leidesdorff," New Helvetia, March 25, 1848, in *Letters of the Gold Discovery, Keepsake Series.* 4 p. This series was edited by GPH for the Book Club of California; see under EDITORIAL.

1949 *Campaigns in the West, 1856–1861. The Journal and Letters of Colonel John Van Deusen Du Bois, with pencil sketches by Joseph Heger*, Tucson, Arizona, printed at the Grabhorn Press for the Arizona Pioneers Historical Society, 1949. xii, 120 (3) p. (300 copies printed.)

1949 GPH and Edgar F. Goad, *A Scientist on the Trail. Travel Letters of A. F. Bandelier, 1880–1881*, Quivira Society Publications, X, Berkeley, 1949. xi, 142 p. (500 copies printed.) Originally announced for publication in June, 1940, this work was delayed by World War II. Goad died prematurely in 1947, and in consequence the introduction as well as the preface was written by GPH, who also translated some of the letters from the German.

1949 *The Treaty of Guadalupe Hidalgo, February Second 1848* [Bancroft Library Publications No. 1]. Berkeley, the Friends of the Bancroft Library, 1949. 79 p. (500 copies printed at the Grabhorn Press.)

1950 GPH and Edward H. Howes, *Overland to California on the Southwestern Trail, 1849. Diary of Robert Eccleston.* Berkeley and Los Angeles, 1950. xvii, 256 p. [Bancroft Library Publications No. 2]. (750 copies printed for the Friends of the Bancroft Library by Lawton Kennedy, the Westgate Press, Oakland.)

1950 "Manuscript Collections in the Bancroft Library," *The Amer-*

ican Archivist, January, 1950 (13: 1: 15–26). A paper read in slightly different form at the annual meeting of the Society of American Archivists in 1947.

1951   *Teritory of Utah vs. Thomas Oudercark, Almon Colvin, James Loyd*, Oakland, [Lawton Kennedy in] The Westgate Press, 1951. [4] p. A document of April 11, 1855, reproduced in facsimile with introductory note on "Frontier Justice" by GPH and a note at end: "Perpetrated for the joy of the doing and the amazement of his fellow Roxburghers in the month of May, 1951."

1951   *The Larkin Papers. Personal, Business, and Official Correspondence of Thomas Oliver Larkin, Merchant and United States Consul in California. Volume I, 1822–1842.* Berkeley and Los Angeles, 1951. xxxi, 352 p. The succeeding nine volumes have the same subtitle and are described by short title.

1952   *The Larkin Papers. . . . Volume II. 1843–1844.* Berkeley and Los Angeles, 1952. xxii, 362 p.

1952   *The Larkin Papers. . . . Volume III. 1845.* Berkeley and Los Angeles, 1952. xxvi, 372 p.

1952   "Oñate's Effort to Gain Political Autonomy for New Mexico," *HAHR*, August, 1952 (32: 3: 321–330). Also printed separately.

1953   Foreword to Doris Marion Wright, *A Guide to the Mariano Guadalupe Vallejo Documentos para la Historia de California, 1780–1875*, Berkeley and Los Angeles, 1953. 264 p. Half-title: Guides to the Manuscript Collections in the Bancroft Library of the University of California. 1. The Vallejo Papers.

1953   *The Larkin Papers. . . . Volume IV. 1845–1846.* Berkeley and Los Angeles, 1953. xxxi, 411 p.

1953   GPH and Agapito Rey, *Don Juan de Oñate, Colonizer of New Mexico, 1595–1628.* 2 vols., xvi, 1187 p. Coronado Cuarto Centennial Publications, V-VI, Albuquerque, 1953.

1953   GPH, with James F. King, Lawrence Kinnaird, and Engel Sluiter, "Herbert Eugene Bolton, 1870–1953," *HAHR*, February, 1953 (33: 1: 184–186).

1953   "In Memoriam: Herbert Eugene Bolton, 1870–1953," *The*

Americas, April, 1953 (9: 4: 391–398). Also printed separately.

1954 *A Facsimile Edition of California's First Book, Reglamento Provic-ional, Printed at Monterey in 1834 by Agustin V. Zamorano. Trans-lated by Ramon Ruiz & Theresa Vigil. A Note on the Printing [by] George L. Harding. An Historical Note [by] George P. Hammond.* San Francisco, Book Club of California, 1954. 16 p. (400 copies designed and printed by Lawton Kennedy.)

1955 *The Larkin Papers.... Volume V. 1846.* Berkeley and Los Angeles, 1955. xxviii, 333 p.

1955 Introduction to *On the Ambitious Projects of Russia in regard to North West America, with Particular Reference to New Albion & New California, by an Englishman. 1830.* San Francisco, Book Club of California, 1955. 79 p. (350 copies printed by the Allen Press.)

1956 "The Search for the Fabulous in the Settlement of the South-west," *UHQ*, January, 1956 (24: 1: 1–19). Also printed sepa-rately.

1956 *Romance of the California Ranchos*, n. p., 1956. 12 p. Cover-title.

1956 "Gaspar de Villagrá's Historia de la Nueva México," a treasure from the Bancroft Library, selected by George P. Hammond, *Treasures of California Collections*, No. 4, San Francisco; printed by Lawton Kennedy for the Book Club of California, 1956. 4 p. Keepsake Series.

1956 "Eleanor Bancroft, a Tribute," in Antiquarian Booksellers' Association of America, Southern California Chapter, *Bulletin No. 1*, Van Nuys, 1956, pp. 3–4.

1957 "Eleanor Ashby Bancroft," *HAHR*, February, 1957 (37: 1: 153).

1957 "The Date of Oñate's Return from New Mexico," *El Palacio*, May–June, 1957 (64: 5–6: 142–144).

1957 GPH and Agapito Rey, "The Crown's Participation in the Founding of New Mexico," *NMHR*, October, 1957 (32: 4: 293–309). Also printed separately.

1957 "Henry Raup Wagner, 1862–1957," *HAHR*, November, 1957 (37: 4: 486–488). Accompanied by a "select bibliography" of

Wagner's writings in the Latin American field, prepared by Jerry E. Patterson. Also printed separately; and see under TITLES ANNOUNCED FOR EARLY PUBLICATION.

1958   *Noticias de California, First Report of the Occupation by the Portolá Expedition, 1770,* San Francisco, the Book Club of California, 1958. 53 p. (400 copies printed.)

1958   "Berkeley," *Encyclopaedia Britannica.* (Written in 1958; printed in subsequent editions.)

1959   *The Larkin Papers. . . . Volume VI. 1847.* Berkeley and Los Angeles, 1959. xxx, 361 p.

1959   *The Duchow Journal; a voyage from Boston to California, 1852.* San Francisco, printed and published by Mallette Dean, 1959. [64] p. (200 copies "laid out at the Allen Press, Kentfield, California.")

1959   *Sir Francis Drake and the Finding of the Plate of Brass Now in the Bancroft Library, University of California.* [Berkeley, 1959. 4 p.] Of this leaflet, printed by Lawton Kennedy, there have been two subsequent printings, with slight changes.

1959   *Letters from Thomas Oliver Larkin to his Wife Rachel, written during his imprisonment as a hostage, November, 1846, to January, 1847,* Bohemian Grove, California, Silverado Squatters' Camp, 1959. 20 p.

1959   "New Mexico," *American Educator Encyclopedia.* (Written in 1959; printed in subsequent editions.)

1959   "Coronado, Francisco Vasquez de," *Encyclopaedia Britannica.* (Written in 1959; printed in subsequent editions.)

1959   "The Americas," *Encyclopaedia Britannica.* (Written in 1959; printed in subsequent editions.)

1960   "Bolton, Herbert Eugene," *Encyclopaedia Britannica.* (Written in 1960; printed in subsequent editions.)

1960   *The Larkin Papers. . . . Volume VII. 1847–1848.* Berkeley and Los Angeles, 1960. xxviii, 369 p.

1960   "Coronado, Francisco Vasquez de," *Collier's Encyclopedia.* (Written in 1960; printed in subsequent editions.)

1960   "Appreciation" of Carl I. Wheat, in George L. Harding, *The*

Published Writings of Carl Irving Wheat, San Francisco, The Roxburghe Club of San Francisco and the Zamorano Club of Los Angeles, 1960. ix, 20 [1] p. (350 copies printed.)

1962   *The Larkin Papers. . . . Volume VIII. 1848–1851.* Berkeley and Los Angeles, 1962. xxix, 420 p.

1963   *The Larkin Papers. . . . Volume IX. 1851–1853.* Berkeley and Los Angeles, 1963. xxi, 320 p.

1963   GPH and Dale L. Morgan, *A Guide to the Manuscript Collections of the Bancroft Library,* Berkeley and Los Angeles, 1963. vii, 379 p. Half title: Bancroft Library Publications, Bibliographical Series, Volume I, Pacific and Western Manuscripts (except California).

1963   Foreword to Gloria G. Cline, *Exploring the Great Basin,* Norman, Oklahoma, 1963. xviii, 254 p.

1964   *The Larkin Papers. . . . Volume X. 1854–1858.* Berkeley and Los Angeles, 1964. xxxv, 353 p.

1964   *Who Saw the Elephant? An Inquiry by a Scholar Well Acquainted with the Beast.* San Francisco, California Historical Society, 1964. 13 p. (250 copies printed by the Tamalpais Press.) Revised from an address delivered before the California Library Association as the Edith M. Coulter Lecture, October 17, 1957.

TITLES ANNOUNCED FOR EARLY PUBLICATION

A. GPH and Agapito Rey, *The Rediscovery of New Mexico, 1580–1594,* Coronado Cuarto Centennial Publications, III.

B. Introduction to Henry R. Wagner, *The Life and Writings of Bartolomé de las Casas.* (The introduction, "Henry Raup Wagner, 1862–1957," with minor revisions is the monograph printed in *Hispanic American Historical Review,* November, 1957. See above.)

C. GPH and Dale L. Morgan, *Captain Charles M. Weber, Pioneer of the San Joaquin and Founder of Stockton.*

D. GPH and Gwladys Williams, *A Guide to the Manuscript Collections of the Bancroft Library. Volume II. Mexican and Spanish Colonial American Manuscripts.*

E.   *Gold Digging Without a Shovel. Letters of Daniel Wadsworth Coit, from Mexico and California, 1848–1851.*

F.   Introduction to James Madison Cutts, *The Conquest of California and New Mexico, by the Forces of the United States, in the Years 1846 & 1847* [originally published at Philadelphia, 1847].

BOOK REVIEWS

1924   Hackett, "Historical Documents Relating to New Mexico (Volume I)," (Washington, 1923), *SWHQ*, April, 1924 (27: 4: 329–333).

1924   Peck, "Industrial and Commercial South America" (New York, 1922), University of North Dakota *Quarterly Journal*, November, 1924 (15: 1: 73–74).

1931   Bolton, "Anza's California Expeditions" (Berkeley, 1930), *SWHQ*, July, 1931 (35: 1: 83–86).

1932   Mason, "Columbus Came Late" (New York, 1931), *PHR*, September, 1932 (1: 3: 374–376).

1932   Thomas, "Forgotten Frontiers" (Norman, Oklahoma, 1932), *CHSQ*, December, 1932 (11: 4: 387–388).

1932   Hewett, "Ancient Life in the American Southwest" (Indianapolis, 1930), *PHR*, December, 1932 (1: 4: 491–492).

1934   Wilgus, "Modern Hispanic America" (Washington, 1933), *PHR*, December, 1934 (3: 4: 455–457).

1935   Bloom and Donnelly, "New Mexico History and Civics" (Albuquerque, 1933), *PHR*, June, 1935 (4: 2: 185–186).

1936   Thomas, "After Coronado" (Norman, Oklahoma, 1935), *PHR*, March, 1936 (5: 1: 83–84).

1937   Jones, "Coronado and Quivira" (Lyons, Kansas, 1937), *NMHR*, October, 1937 (12: 4: 455–456).

1938   Hackett, "Historical Documents Relating to New Mexico (Volume III)," (Washington, 1937), *SWHQ*, April, 1938 (41: 4: 360–361).

1938   Castañeda, "Our Catholic Heritage in Texas (Volumes I–II)," (Austin, 1936), *PHR*, June, 1938 (7: 2: 170–172).

1938   Lockwood, "The Apache Indians," (New York, 1938), *PHR*, September, 1938 (7: 3: 278).

1939 Castañeda, "Our Catholic Heritage in Texas (Volume III)" (Austin, 1938), *PHR*, March, 1939 (8: 1: 124).

1940 Robinson, "Ranchos Become Cities" (Pasadena, 1939), *HAHR*, February, 1940 (20: 1: 128–129).

1940 Hallenbeck, "Cabeza de Vaca" (Glendale, 1940), *PHR*, December, 1940 (9: 4: 471–472).

1941 Vestal, "The Old Santa Fe Trail" (Boston, 1939), *HAHR*, May, 1941 (21: 2: 317–318).

1941 Hafen and Rister, "Western America" (New York, 1941), *NMHR*, October, 1941 (16: 4: 432–433).

1941 Foreman, "A Pathfinder in the Southwest" (Norman, Oklahoma, 1941), *HAHR*, November, 1941 (21: 4: 642–643).

1941 Long, "Piñon Country" (New York, 1941), *PHR*, December, 1941 (10: 4: 495–496).

1941 Pinchon, "Zapata, the Unconquerable" (New York, 1941), *PHR*, December, 1941 (10: 4: 487).

1942 Day, "Coronado's Quest" (Berkeley, 1940), *HAHR*, February, 1942 (22: 1: 141–142).

1942 Wilgus, "Hispanic American Essays: A Memorial to James Alexander Robertson" (Chapel Hill, 1942), *PHR*, December, 1942 (11: 4: 451).

1943 Wright, "My Rambles as East Texas Cowboy" (Austin, 1942), and Perry, "Texas, a World in Itself" (New York, 1942), *MVHR*, March, 1943 (29: 4: 597–598).

1943 Bieber and Hafen, "The Southwest Historical Series," Index Volume (Glendale, 1943), *MVHR*, September, 1943 (30: 2: 269–270).

1945 Biesanz and Biesanz, "Costa Rican Life" (New York, 1944), *PHR*, June, 1945 (14: 2: 237–238).

1945 Ganaway, "New Mexico and the Sectional Controversy" (Albuquerque, 1944), *MVHR*, December, 1945 (32: 3: 459–460).

1947 Martínez Del Río, "Tlatelolco a través de los tiempos" (Mexico, 1944–1945), *HAHR*, May, 1947 (27: 2: 344–345).

1948 Pomeroy, "The Territories and the United States" (Philadelphia, 1947), *HAHR*, February, 1948 (28: 1: 123).

1948   Hackett, "Pichardo's Treatise on the Limits of Louisiana and Texas (Volume IV)," (Austin, 1946), *HAHR*, May, 1948 (28: 2: 242–243).

1948   Rader, "South of Forty" (Norman, Oklahoma, 1947), *PHR*, May, 1948 (17: 2: 209–210).

1949   Shinn, "Mining Camps" (New York, 1948), *AHR*, January, 1949 (54: 2: 451).

1949   Chamberlain, "The Conquest and Colonization of Yucatan, 1517–1550" (Washington, 1948), *HAHR*, November, 1949 (29: 4: 586–587).

1949   Cleland, "Apron Full of Gold" (San Marino, 1949), *MVHR*, December, 1949 (36: 3: 520–521).

1951   Maximin Piette, "Le Secret de Junípero Serra" (Washington and Brussels, 1949), *HAHR*, May, 1951 (31: 2: 305–306).

1951   Martínez, "Icazbalceta: His Place in Mexican Historiography" (Washington, 1947), *AHR*, October, 1951 (57: 1: 271–272).

1952   Fergusson, "New Mexico: A Pageant of Three Peoples" (New York, 1951), *AHR*, July, 1952 (57: 4: 1066–1067).

1952   Phares, "Cavalier in the Wilderness" (Baton Rouge, 1952), *MVHR*, December, 1952 (39: 3: 536–537).

1955   James, "Three Years Among the Indians and Mexicans" (Chicago, 1953), *HAHR*, February, 1955 (35: 1: 148–149).

1955   Hafen and Hafen, "Old Spanish Trail: Santa Fe to Los Angeles" (Glendale, 1954), *AHR*, April, 1955 (40: 3: 704–705).

1956   Herrera, "Historia de la Nueva Mexico" (Madrid, 1953), *HAHR*, February, 1956 (36: 1: 139).

1956   Castañeda and Dabbs, "Independent Mexico in Documents" (Mexico, 1954), *HAHR*, August, 1956 (36: 3: 404–405).

1957   Adams and Chávez, "[Domínguez:] The Missions of New Mexico, 1776" *PHR*, February, 1957 (26: 1: 69–71).

1958   Gladwin, "A History of the Ancient Southwest" (Portland, Maine, 1957), *AHR*, January, 1958 (63: 2: 429–430).

1959   Moorhead, "New Mexico's Royal Road" (Norman, Oklahoma, 1958), *NMHR*, April, 1959 (34: 2: 154–156).

1959   "Sinopsis bibliográfica mexicana" (Mexico, 1958), *HAHR*, May, 1959 (39: 2: 352).

1959   Lorenzana, "Viage de Hernán Cortés a la peninsula de Californias" (Madrid, 1958), *HAHR*, August, 1959 (39: 3: 487).

1960   Simpson, "The San Sabá Papers" (San Francisco, 1960), *CHSQ*,
September, 1960 (39: 3: 271–272).

1960   Brigham, "Fifty Years of Collecting Americana" (Worcester,
1958), *PNWQ*, January, 1960 (51: 1: 36).

1961   Forbes, "Apache, Navaho and Spaniard" (Norman, Oklahoma,
1960), *AHR*, July, 1961 (66: 4: 1128).

1964   Nunis, "Josiah Belden, Memoir and Early Letters" (George-
town, California, 1962), *SCQ*, June, 1964 (46: 2: 182–183).

EDITORIAL

Under this head are described titles, or groups of titles, for which
George P. Hammond has had a broad responsibility transcending the
role of author or annotator, frequently with the title of "general editor" or "managing editor." Individual titles to which he made contributions in his own name are also described under GENERAL PUB-
LICATIONS above.

QUIVIRA SOCIETY PUBLICATIONS

I.   *Expedition into New Mexico Made by Antonio de Espejo, 1582–1583,
as Revealed in the Journal of Diego Pérez de Luxán, a Member of the
Party. Translated, with Introduction and Notes, by George Peter
Hammond . . . and Agapito Rey* . . . Los Angeles, The Quivira
Society, 1929. 143 p. (500 copies printed, 30 on large paper.)

II. *The Indian Uprising in Lower California, 1734–1737, as Described
by Father Sigismundo Taraval. Translated, with Introduction and
Notes, by Marguerite Eyer Wilbur.* Los Angeles, The Quivira
Society, 1931. xii, 298 p. (665 copies printed.)

III. *The Mercurio Volante of Don Carlos de Sigüenza y Góngora. An
Account of the First Expedition of Don Diego de Vargas into New
Mexico in 1692. Translated, with Introduction and Notes, by Irving
Albert Leonard* . . . Los Angeles, The Quivira Society, 1932.
136 p. (665 copies printed.)

IV. *History of New Mexico, by Gaspar Pérez de Villagrá, Alcalá, 1610.
Translated by Gilberto Espinosa. Introduction and Notes by F. W.*

Hodge. Los Angeles, The Quivira Society, 1933. 308 p. (665 copies printed.)

V. *Diary of the Alarcón Expedition into Texas, 1718–1719, by Fray Francisco Céliz. Translated by Fritz Leo Hoffmann.* Los Angeles, The Quivira Society, 1935. 124 p. (600 copies printed, of which 100 have a 52-page facsimile insert of the handwritten original).

VI. *History of Texas, 1673–1779, by Fray Juan Agustín Morfí, Missionary, Teacher, Historian. Translated, with Biographical Introduction and Annotations, by Carlos Eduardo Castañeda* . . . Albuquerque, The Quivira Society, 1935. 2 vols., 496 p. (500 copies printed.)

VII. *The Spanish Southwest, 1542–1794. An Annotated Bibliography by Henry R. Wagner* . . . Albuquerque, The Quivira Society, 1937. 2 vols., 553 p. (401 copies printed.)

VIII. *New Mexico in 1602. Juan de Montoya's Relation of the Discovery of New Mexico. [Translated and edited by] George P. Hammond and Agapito Rey.* Albuquerque, The Quivira Society, 1938. 143 p. (550 copies printed.)

IX. *Spanish Approach to Pensacola, 1689–1693. Translated, with Introduction and Notes, by Irving A. Leonard . . . Foreword by James A. Robertson* . . . Albuquerque, The Quivira Society, 1939. xvii, 323 p. (550 copies printed.)

X. *A Scientist on the Trail. Travel Letters of A. F. Bandelier, 1880–1881. [Edited by] George P. Hammond and Edgar F. Goad.* Berkeley, The Quivira Society, 1949. xi, 142 p. (500 copies printed.)

XI. *Three New Mexico Chronicles. The* Exposicion *of Don Pedro Bautista Pino, 1812; the* Ojeada *of Lic. Antonio Barreiro, 1832; and the additions by Don José Agustín de Escudero, 1849. Translated, wtih Introduction and Notes, by H. Bailey Carroll [and] J. Villasana Haggard.* Albuquerque, The Quivira Society, 1942. xxi, 342 (*i.e.*, 344) p. (557 copies printed.)

XII. *Instructions for Governing the Interior Provinces of New Spain, 1786, by Bernardo de Gálvez. Translated and Edited by Donald E. Worcester* . . . Berkeley, The Quivira Society, 1951. xiii, 150 p. (500 copies printed.)

XIII. *The Frontiers of New Spain. Nicolás de Lafora's Description, 1766–*

1768. [*Translated and edited by*] *Lawrence Kinnaird*. Berkeley, The Quivira Society, 1958. xviii, 243 p. (400 copies printed.)

Publications of the New Mexico Historical Records Survey

From 1936 to 1939 George P. Hammond was State Director of the New Mexico Historical Records Survey, Works Progress Administration (afterward renamed Work Projects Administration). The primary task of the H. R. S. was to compile inventories of the records of the various counties. The counties were numbered according to alphabetical order, but inventories were published as they were completed, regardless of numerical position. The suspension of the Historical Records Survey in 1942, after the United States entered World War II, led also to the suspension of the publication program, and many of the inventories never appeared. Altogether, fifteen New Mexico county inventories were published (besides some other titles not here germane). The first five had prefaces signed by George P. Hammond as State Director; the others were signed by his successors, Herbert O. Brayer and G. Robert Massey. The completed inventories are for Bernalillo, Colfax, Doña Ana, Eddy, Grant, Hidalgo, Luna, Mora, Otero, Sandoval, San Miguel, Sierra, Torrance, Union, and Valencia counties. Described below in chronological order are the five titles here pertinent, all of them mimeographed.

Inventory of the County Archives of New Mexico. Prepared by The Historical Records Survey, Divison of Women's and Professional Service Projects, Works Progress Administration. No. 4. Colfax County (Raton). Albuquerque, The Historical Records Survey, November, 1937. 94 p. (Cover is dated December, 1937.) Preface dated November, 1937.

Inventory of the County Archives of New Mexico. Prepared by the Historical Records Survey. . . . No. 1. Bernalillo County (Albuquerque). Albuquerque, The Historical Records Survey, September, 1938. 255 p. Preface dated September, 1938.

Inventory of the County Archives of New Mexico. Prepared by the Historical Records Survey. . . . No. 23. Sandoval County (Bernalillo). Albuquerque, The Historical Records Survey, January, 1939. 180 p. Preface dated January, 1939.

Inventory of the County Archives of New Mexico. Prepared by the Historical Records Survey, Division of Professional and Service Projects, Works Progress Administration. No. 29. Torrance County (Estancia). Albuquerque, The Historical Records Survey, April, 1939. 181 p. Preface dated February, 1939.

Inventory of the County Archives of New Mexico. Prepared by the Historical Records Survey. . . . No. 8. Eddy County (Carlsbad). Albuquerque, The Historical Records Survey, May, 1939. 213 p. Preface dated May, 1939.

Coronado Cuarto Centennial Publications

These publications were inaugurated in 1940 by the Cuarto Centennial Commission and the University of New Mexico, under the general editorship of George P. Hammond. What may be described as the "Coronado Series" was to consist of twelve volumes. As a result of the death or disability of the authors, not all volumes originally announced were written, and changes were made. As of March, 1965, ten have been published, one is in press, and one is still in preparation. In the companion "Bandelier Series" only one title has been published.

[Coronado Series]

I. *Coronado on the Turquoise Trail, Knight of Pueblos and Plains,* by Herbert E. Bolton. Albuquerque, The University of New Mexico Press, 1949. xvi, 491 p.

II. *Narratives of the Coronado Expedition, 1540–1542.* [*Edited and translated by*] George P. Hammond . . . *and Agapito Rey* . . . Albuquerque, The University of New Mexico Press, 1940. xii, 413 p.

III. [*The Rediscovery of New Mexico, 1580–1594, by George P. Hammond and Agapito Rey.* In press.]

IV. *Fray Alonso de Benavides' Revised Memorial of 1634. With Numerous Supplementary Documents Elaborately Annotated.* [*Edited and translated by*] Frederick Webb Hodge, George P. Hammond [*and*] Agapito Rey. Albuquerque, The University of New Mexico Press, 1945. xvi, 368 p.

V-VI. *Don Juan de Oñate, Colonizer of New Mexico, 1595–1628.* [*Edited and translated by*] George P. Hammond . . . [*and*] Agapito Rey . . . Albuquerque, The University of New Mexico Press, 1953. 2 vols., xvi, 1187 p.

VII. [*New Mexico in the Latter Seventeenth Century, by France V. Scholes.* In preparation.]

VIII-IX. *Revolt of the Pueblo Indians of New Mexico and Otermín's Attempted Reconquest, 1680–1682. Introduction and Annotations by Charles Wilson Hackett . . . Translations of Original Documents by Charmion Clair Shelby* . . . Albuquerque, The University of New Mexico Press, 1942. 2 vols., ccx, 262; xii, 430 p.

X. *First Expedition of Vargas into New Mexico, 1692. Translated, with Introduction and Notes, by J. Manuel Espinosa* . . . Albuquerque, The University of New Mexico Press, 1940. x, 319 p.

XI. *The Plains Indians and New Mexico, 1751–1778. A Collection of Documents Illustrative of the History of the Eastern Frontier of New Mexico.* [*Edited and translated by*] *Alfred Barnaby Thomas* . . . Albuquerque, The University of New Mexico Press, 1940. 232 p.

XII. *Ignaz Pfefferkorn, Sonora, a Description of the Province. Translated and Annotated by Theodore E. Treutlein* . . . Albuquerque, The University of New Mexico Press, 1949. xv, 329 p.

BANDELIER SERIES

Pioneers in American Anthropology: The Bandelier-Morgan Letters, 1873–1883 [*edited by*] *Leslie A. White* . . . [*and with a foreword by GPH*] Albuquerque, The University of New Mexico Press, 1940. 2 vols., [xv], 272; [vi], 266 p. (400 copies printed.) According to an end note, the printing was completed in Albuquerque August 6, 1940, "the one hundredth anniversary of the birth of Adolph F. Bandelier."

MISCELLANEOUS PUBLICATIONS

New Spain and the Anglo-American West. Historical Contributions Presented to Herbert Eugene Bolton. Los Angeles, Privately Printed, 1932. [Copyrighted by George P. Hammond. Printed by the Lancaster Press, Inc.,

Lancaster, Pa.] 2 vols., xii, 333; [ii], 277 p. (500 copies printed.) The elevation of Herbert E. Bolton to the office of vice-president of the American Historical Association in 1930 suggested to some of his students a volume of historical contributions, to be presented on the occasion of his presidential address in 1932. Two volumes resulted, one dealing with the northward advance of the frontiers of New Spain, the other with the American westward movement. Volume I, "New Spain," was edited by Charles W. Hackett, George P. Hammond, and J. Lloyd Mecham (it includes a contribution by GPH on Oñate listed under GENERAL PUBLICATIONS). Volume II, "The Anglo-American West," was edited by William C. Binkley, Cardinal Goodwin, and J. Fred Rippy.

The Historian. Scholarly journal founded by Phi Alpha Theta, national history fraternity, with George P. Hammond as editor, Autumn, 1938–Autumn, 1946 (Vol. 1, No. 1, to Vol. 9, No. 1, issued semi-annually). During and for some years after GPH's tenure as editor, the journal was printed at Albuquerque. The seventeen numbers he edited contain one article by him, published in 1945 (see under GENERAL PUBLICATIONS), and occasional signed and unsigned "editor's page" comments.

Motolinía's History of the Indians of New Spain. Translated and edited by Elizabeth Andros Foster . . . Albuquerque, 1950. 294 p. (500 copies printed.) This work was issued with the half title: "Documents and Narratives Concerning the Discovery & Conquest of Latin America, New Series, Number Four, Published by The Cortés Society, Bancroft Library, Berkeley, California." The Cortés Society originally flourished in New York City, 1917–1924. After a moribund period, it was revived at the Bancroft Library in 1939 to publish documents concerned with Hispanic American history, and printed three monographs by Henry R. Wagner, which appeared in 1941, 1942, and 1944. The second of these volumes listed as the Society's council Herbert Ingram Priestley, Thomas Winthrop Streeter, and Henry Raup Wagner. The third volume, issued after Priestley's death, named a council consisting of Arthur Scott Aiton, Eleanor Bancroft, Thomas Winthrop Streeter, and Henry Raup Wagner. The fourth and final publication of the revived Cortés Society, listed, in addition, G. R. G. Conway as council member and George P. Hammond as managing editor. The translator of *Motolinía* thanks GPH for suggesting the need of such a work, and for helping in preparing the manuscript for the press. *The Larkin Papers* . . . Berkeley and Los Angeles, Printed for the Bancroft Library by the University of California Press, 1951–1964. The ten volumes comprising this series, edited by George P. Hammond, are individually described above. An eleventh (index) volume is contemplated.

Letters of the Gold Discovery. . . . *Published for its members, by the Book Club of California. 1948.* Keepsake Series, edited by George P. Hammond; 12 parts in slide case.

This series, issued monthly during 1948, consisted of the following:

1. Caroline Wenzel, "Captain John A. Sutter Lord of New Helvetia" (letters to George McKinstry, Jun., New Helvetia, January 15 and 23, 1848).
2. Charles Olson, "The Sutter-Marshall Lease with the Yalesumney Indians for Monopoly of the Gold-Bearing Lands" (February 4, 1848).
3. George P. Hammond, "Sutter to Leidesdorff" (New Helvetia, March 25, 1848).
4. George L. Harding, "Edward C. Kemble to John S. Hittell" (New York, October 6, 1885).
5. Rodman W. Paul, "A Letter from Thomas O. Larkin to Governor R. B. Mason" (Pueblo de San José, May 25, 1848).
6. Robert G. Cleland, "W. D. M. Howard of San Francisco to B. T. Reed of Boston" (San Francisco, June 11, 1848).
7. Reuben L. Underhill, "Consul Thomas O. Larkin to Secretary of State James Buchanan" (Monterey, July 20, 1848).
8. Neal Harlow, "Letter of Captain J. L. Folsom to the Secretary of the National Institute at Washington, D. C." (San Francisco, August 29, 1848).
9. Robert J. Parker, "Letter of Ebenezer Larkin Childs from Washington, D. C. to Thomas O. Larkin, Monterey, California" (September 27, 1848).

10. Joseph Henry Jackson, "Rodman M. Price, New York, to Thomas O. Larkin, Monterey, California" (October 18, 1848).
11. Adele Ogden, "A Letter from Stephen Reynolds of Honolulu to Thomas O. Larkin of San Francisco" (November 12, 1848).
12. Oscar Lewis, "Robert Semple of Benicia City to Thomas O. Larkin at Monterey" (December 13, 1848).

Each 4-page Keepsake contains a separate facsimile of the document.

PUBLICATIONS OF THE FRIENDS OF THE BANCROFT LIBRARY

Two years after the Friends came into being, they were greeted in print by H. H. Bancroft's son Philip with an address on his father, and in the same month, September, 1948, the Friends sent out their first *Annual Letter*. Next year, the Friends inaugurated their publication program with a distinguished volume, *The Treaty of Guadalupe Hidalgo,* edited by George P. Hammond as described above (and below). *Bancroftiana* launched upon its cheerfully irregular course early in 1950, and since then the Friends have maintained a consistent and varied publication program, under the general editorship of George P. Hammond (except that Dr. James D. Hart assumed responsibility as Acting Director during the academic year 1961–1962, when GPH was in Europe on sabbatical leave). The various publications are classed in groups for description here.

PERIODICAL PUBLICATIONS

Bancroftiana "Published occasionally by the Friends of the Bancroft Library, University of California, Berkeley 4, California"; includes many contributions by GPH, signed and unsigned. The first number, of 6 pages, was dated March, 1950. Through March, 1965, thirty-six numbers have appeared, each from 4 to 8 pages, dated March, June, December, 1950; May, December, 1951; May, December, 1952; May, October, 1953; May, December, 1954; May, December, 1955; May, November, 1956; April, November, 1957; April, November, 1958; April, October, December, 1959; April, November, 1960; March, June, November, 1961; April, June, November, 1962; April, June, December, 1963; April, November, 1964; March, 1965. A thirty-seventh number is contemplated for June, 1965, with an index for all issues published during the Hammond directorate.

Annual Letters

Ten printed *Annual Letters* have been addressed to the Friends, dated and signed by the Chairman as follows:

September 1, 1948. George L. Harding. Broadside.

November, 1953. William G. Paden. Broadside.

November, 1954. Carl I. Wheat. Broadside.

November, 1955. Carl I. Wheat. Broadside.

November, 1956. Carl I. Wheat. Broadside.

May, 1957. Mrs. Adeline H. Gilchrist; with a description of "The Portolá Documents" and a facsimile page displaying signatures of Costansó, Fages, Rivera, and Portolá; in all, 5 p.

May, 1958. Mrs. Adeline H. Gilchrist. Broadside.

May, 1959. Mrs. Adeline H. Gilchrist. Broadsheet.

May 31, 1960. Mrs. Adeline H. Gilchrist. Broadsheet.

May 31, 1961. O. Cort Majors. Broadsheet.

Addresses

Hubert Howe Bancroft. An Address by His Son Philip Bancroft at the Grove of the Turning Leaves, the Family Farm, September Fifth, 1948. [San Francisco, September, 1948. 22 p.] "Privately printed by Paul Bancroft for his fellow club members of The Family and for 'The Friends of the Bancroft Library.' "

The Bancroft Library—Whence—What—Whither. An address delivered by Carl I. Wheat on May 22, 1955, before the Friends of the Bancroft Library in commemoration of the 50th Anniversary of its acquisition by the University of California. [Eighth Annual Address.] Berkeley, 1955. 18 p.

Material for the Diary of a Great People. An Address by Edgar Eugene Robinson before the Friends of the Bancroft Library, May 1956. Foreword by Carl I. Wheat. [Ninth Annual Address.] Berkeley, 1956. iii, 9 p.

The California Background; Spanish or American? By John D. Hicks. [Tenth Annual Address, delivered before the Friends of the Bancroft Library May 5, 1957.] Berkeley [1957]. 18, [1] p.

Landscapes and Bookscapes of California. An Address by Lawrence Clark Powell. [Eleventh Annual Address, delivered before the Friends of the Bancroft Library, May 4, 1958. Berkeley, 1958]. 15 p.

The Changing Responsibilities of a United States Senator. An Address by William Fife Knowland. [Twelfth Annual Address delivered before the Friends of the Bancroft Library, May 3, 1959. Berkeley, 1959.] 10 p. Includes, pp. 9–10, letters sent Mr. Knowland by former Senate colleagues, May 7–12, 1959, commenting on his address.

GENERAL PUBLICATIONS AND KEEPSAKES

The Treaty of Guadalupe Hidalgo, February Second, 1848. Edited by George P. Hammond. Berkeley, the Friends of the Bancroft Library [1949]. [v], 79 p. [Bancroft Library Publications, No. 1.] (500 copies printed at the Grabhorn Press, San Francisco, February, 1949.)

Overland to California on the Southwestern Trail, 1849. Diary of Robert Eccleston. Edited by George P. Hammond and Edward H. Howes. Berkeley and Los Angeles, University of California Press, 1950. xvii, 256 p. [Bancroft Library Publications, No. 2.] (750 copies printed.)

A Description of California in 1828, by José Bandini. Translated by Doris Marion Wright. Berkeley, Friends of the Bancroft Library, 1951. viii, 52 p. [Bancroft Library Publications, No. 3.] (400 copies printed by the Westgate Press.)

The Opening of the California Trail. The Story of the Stevens Party from the reminiscences of Moses Schallenberger as set down for H. H. Bancroft about 1885, edited and expanded by Horace S. Foote in 1888, and now edited with Introduction, notes, maps, and illustrations by George R. Stewart. Berkeley, University of California Press, 1953. vii, 115 p. [Bancroft Library Publications, No. 4.] (350 copies specially bound for the Friends of the Bancroft Library from an edition published by the University of California Press.)

Ramblings in California. The Adventures of Henry Cerruti. Edited by Margaret Mollins and Virginia E. Thickens. Berkeley, Friends of the Bancroft Library, 1954. 143 p. [Bancroft Library Publications, No. 5.] (500 copies printed by the Gillick Press, Berkeley, California.)

The Mariposa Indian War, 1850–1851. Diaries of Robert Eccleston; The California Gold Rush, Yosemite, and the High Sierra. Edited by C. Gregory

Crampton. Salt Lake City, University of Utah Press, 1957. vii, 168 p. [Bancroft Library Publications, No. 6.] (500 copies printed for the Friends of the Bancroft Library by the University of Utah Press, November, 1957.)

Stockton Boyhood. Being the Reminiscences of Carl Ewald Grunsky, which cover the years from 1855 to 1877. Edited by Clotilde Grunsky Taylor. Berkeley, the Friends of the Bancroft Library, 1959. iii, 134 p. [Bancroft Library Publications, No. 7.] (800 copies designed and printed by Lawton Kennedy.)

American Images of Spanish California [*by*] *James D. Hart.* Berkeley, the Friends of the Bancroft Library [1960]. vi, 39 p. [Bancroft Library Publications, No. 8.] Expanded from the Annual Address delivered before the Friends of the Bancroft Library, May, 1960. (Designed by Roger Levenson; printed by the Howell-North Press, Berkeley.)

The Ralston-Fry Wedding and the Wedding Journey to Yosemite, May 20, 1858. From the Diary of Miss Sarah Haight [*Mrs. Edward Tompkins*] *edited by Francis P. Farquhar.* Berkeley, the Friends of the Bancroft Library, 1961. 24 p. [Bancroft Library Publications, No. 9.] (Printed by the Grabhorn Press.)

Mexico: Ancient and Modern. As represented by a selection of works in the Bancroft Library. An Exhibition Celebrating the Acquisition of the Silvestre Terrazas Collection. Berkeley, the Friends of the Bancroft Library, 1962. 95 p. [Bancroft Library Publications, No. 10.] (Designed and printed by Lawton Kennedy.)

Rose, or Rose Thorn? Three Women of Spanish California. [*By*] *Susanna Bryant Dakin.* Berkeley, the Friends of the Bancroft Library, 1963. x, 60 p. [Friends of the Bancroft Library, Keepsakes, No. 11.] Expanded from the Annual Address delivered before the Friends of the Bancroft Library in May, 1963. (Designed and printed by Lawton Kennedy.)

A Journey to California, 1841. The First Emigrant Party to California by Wagon Train. The Journal of John Bidwell. Introduction by Francis P. Farquhar. Berkeley, the Friends of the Bancroft Library, 1964. [ii], 55, [ii], 32 p. including facsimile of unique Bancroft copy of original edition. ["Number 12 in the series of keepsakes issued by the Friends of the Bancroft Library for its Members."] (Designed and printed by Lawton Kennedy.)

MISCELLANEOUS

The Bancroft Library and Its Friends. An Exhibition commemorating the 100th anniversary of the founding of the Library, The University of California, Berkeley, California, April 23, 1961. 15 p. (Printed by Lawton Kennedy.)

In Remembrance: Edward H. Heller . . . be it resolved that this testimonial of sadness and appreciation be included in the minutes of the meeting of the Council on January 25, 1962 . . . [signed] Council of the Friends of the Bancroft Library. [Berkeley, 1962. Broadside.] (Printed by Lawton Kennedy.)

Women in the West. An Exhibition. Sixteenth Annual Meeting, The Friends of the Bancroft Library, May 5th, 1963. 4 p. (Printed by Lawton Kennedy.)

The Honeyman Collection of Early Californian and Western American Pictorial Material; a Project of The Friends of the Bancroft Library. [Written by Susanna Bryant Dakin.] Berkeley, University of California, Bancroft Library [1963]. 12 p.

G P H's First Appearance in Print: Impressions of Spain in 1923

University of North Dakota Quarterly Journal, November, 1923

Over four and one-quarter centuries ago, three little Spanish cara-
vels came gliding out of the fog and mist of the unknown waters of the
Atlantic, peering at the strange coastline before them. It was the coast
of America, and Christopher Columbus was the knight errant. The
courage of the mutinous and frightened sailors at once revived. As
their heroic commander brandished his sword and took possession of
the land in the name of Castile, their bosoms swelled with pride, exul-
ting over the princely fortunes close at hand. One may well wonder
what dazzling reward the strangers hoped to secure from the greasy,
cinnamon-hued and naked human beings confronting them. The answer is obvious. If it were possible to reach India by sailing west, as
they believed they had done, thereby shattering at a blow the child-
like superstitions of the medieval world, was it not also possible that
they would find the illimitable treasures of Cipango so generally believed to exist? Were not the uncounted treasures of the Great Khan
near at hand, the vastness of which Marco Polo had dangled before
the eyes of Europe two centuries earlier?

In response to the queries of the bearded strangers regarding the
location of Cipango and of the home of the Great Khan, the savages,
unable to comprehend the desires of their guests, pointed elsewhere,
toward the south, west or north. Thus the Spaniards pressed on. The

first little group of one hundred or more men was soon augmented by thousands. They spread north and south as well as west, till the Caribbean was overrun and covered with Spanish settlements. Very soon they spread westward to the mainland, subduing the heathen having the most advanced culture of any in the New World. And there in 1513 another conqueror, engaged in this endless feverish search for the glittering gold, stumbled into the Pacific Ocean. Dashing into its waters, Balboa took possession of all the lands washed by its waters in the name of Castile and Aragon. It was a large order indeed.

In the space of a few years more the great continent of South America was dotted with Spanish and Portuguese settlements, and North America had been occupied as far as the Rio Grande. In the course of the seventeenth century, Spanish New Mexico and then Texas were occupied and colonized in the order named. Hereupon followed a period of consolidation and growth, till, in the middle of the eighteenth century, a most remarkable extension of this great empire took place. The Pacific Coast was colonized from Lower California to San Francisco, which was founded in 1776, and temporary posts were planted on Vancouver Island. In the Mississippi Valley a similar development occurred. Louisiana, which had fallen to Spain at the end of the French and Indian War in 1763, was promptly occupied. So extensive was the influence of Spain that her traders found their way to the villages of the Mandan Indians in North Dakota, not to mention Spain's extensive trade on the Pacific Coast, or her trade with the English colonies to the east, radiating from posts in the Mississippi Valley.

But the rule of Spain is no more. Today her colonies have grown into independent nations. Twenty Hispanic-American nations are abundant proof of the importance of the legacy of Spain and Portugal to the New World, while in our own United States many of our commonwealths revel in the color and lore inherited from Old Spain. These twenty nations are our nearest neighbors, excluding Canada. Our statesmen have continually had to deal with them. The spectre of insurrection or foreign intervention in Hispanic-America has ever haunted our Secretaries of State since President Monroe, just a hundred years ago, declared our friendly interest in their welfare. That interest has never been relaxed. It has, on the contrary, rapidly increased, notably during the past generation. With the acquisition of the Philippines and Puerto Rico in 1898, our inherent spirit of expansion, or manifest destiny, was revealed anew. A virtual protectorate over Cuba followed in due course of time and, shortly thereafter, the Panama Canal was undertaken. Nor could we halt there. In recent years we have assumed additional obligations in these Spanish lands. In Haiti, in Santo Domingo, in Nicaragua, our flag flies, and negotiations with Honduras were carried out, but an agreement failed through rejection by the United States Senate.

Although we have thus for two decades and more been in direct contact with Spanish-speaking nations, we can hardly be said to have achieved great glory. Our officials have had little opportunity to learn their language. Of their history and racial characteristics our government officials have had slight knowledge. As a people we have been ignorant of their life, customs and manners. Such was the situation till recently, and it is still largely true.

There is thus a vast Hispanic-American civilization to the south of us, and in this area new conditions and new problems meet us at every step. Even in the region north of the Rio Grande the imprint of Spanish civilization is unmistakable. From Georgia to California land grants, missions and towns date from the Spanish period. And the literature of the Borderland is tinged with its flavor.

I have thus sketched the story of Spanish expansion on this hemisphere for the reason that it explains the absorbing interest that Spain possesses for the imagination, particularly for those engaged in making known a part of her contribution to the history of the world. The responsibility to make known this story is the work of the historian; only by an appreciation of the continuous historical development of any people can we hope to deal intelligently with them today. Especially is this true where a hurrying and restless American civilization comes in contact with people of different blood, different temperament, different language, and different mode of life. With just such are we conflicting by the extension of our ever-expanding frontier.

The average American citizen is oblivious to the full significance of this movement.

It should at once be observed that Spain is not a homogeneous country. The Cantabrian mountain area of the north with its mining and grazing presents a strange contrast to the lazy and easy-going Andalusia of the south, while the highlands of Castile, the great central grazing region, are equally distinct from the manufacturing sections of the northeast. If we were to examine these individual divisions more closely, we should find as strong a differentiation between the provinces therein as exists in the more general classification. Furthermore, there are four distinct languages in Spain. The Gallegos of the northwest have their own tongue, and the Basques, the Catalonians, and the Castilians likewise. The latter is the national language and is taught in the schools. But the provincial variations persist, and the four mentioned are modified in turn by distinct local development. Such a multitude of differences hinders the development of the nation and continually invites disturbance of the national order.

These elements of disunion have left a strong impress on the Spanish character, and to understand the Spaniard we must needs visit him in his home. It is undoubtedly true that few foreigners fully comprehend him, and the best that we can do is to try. So we begin by traveling in his land, feasting our senses on the ever-changing terrain, and observing the unfamiliar people. If we enter Spain from Paris, we begin to observe a marked change in the actions of those about us as we approach the Pyrenees. Perchance it is a Sunday evening. Our coach is filled with a tumultuous mass of singing, laughing, shouting, and loving people. It is the region of Languedoc, where a hug and a kiss are readily exchanged. Both man and maid, returning from a day of sport in the open, have tasted the vinous nectar, and who shall say which is the more stimulating, the drops of the vine or the spirit and atmosphere of Languedoc? Some of that same spirit reappears south of the French border. Even their dress indicates as much. The brimless little skull-caps worn by our associates of south France persist throughout the highlands of northern Spain. Why? Can one ever cease asking why in this land of strange people, strange customs, and still stranger food?

But let us continue. At midnight we reach the custom-house of

Irun, where friends await us. Our traveling companion, a *Madrileña*, has acquaintances in this village. She is returning from a year of study in America and now, nearing her own country, has lost no time in informing the mayor of the town, a distant friend, of her arrival. So as our baggage is being stacked on the customs counter, the stately gentleman, whose beard has long since renounced any claim on youth, recognizes the *doctora*. Bystanders and officials salute him as he approaches and we, travel-worn and weary, readily submit to his guidance. Under his direction the formality of inspecting the baggage is quickly accomplished and in a few moments we find ourselves in a cab. Our belongings have been tumbled on top of the lone one-horse vehicle, and the happy *cochero,* as he cracks his whip, hurries the unwilling animal over the dark cobblestone streets. Arriving at the hotel we find all in readiness. Ordering a prompt breakfast for the next morning, we soon forget every care as refreshing sleep o'ertakes us.

Arising earlier than the custom of the country sanctions, we make a hurried breakfast of the invariable variety, a cup of chocolate or coffee and a roll, and we are ready for the work of the day. Our route was planned to include the mountainous north as our first objective. It is the region of the sturdy and independent mountaineer from which Spain has recruited many a hero. Let it suffice to mention a Menéndez, the founder of St. Augustine, or an Oñate, the founder of New Mexico. In this harsh region man must struggle to live, and it has nurtured a fine spirit of independence. It was, for instance, the only region unconquered by the Moslems as they swept over Spain into western Europe. As the foreigner gazes on this region, as he observes and compares their municipalities with those familiar to his experience, he is struck by their neatness, cleanliness and modernity. A feeling of disappointment may at times surge through his consciousness that things are not as he thought they would be, that all is marred by the pervading influence of business. Yet it is true. Spain has been infected with the bustle of the demon—business. Her seaports on this coast are progressive, her inland towns are up-to-date, and in some cases the population of these northern centers has practically doubled in the past decade.

Let us take an excursion off the beaten path and invade a mountain village some distance from the coast. The points along the sea are too cosmopolitan; there foreign influence has had its natural effect. We take the train to the point nearest our destination, where an auto stage stands purring, ready to continue the journey. It is a rainy day. A group of soldiers, dressed in their picturesque garb of blue jackets, scarlet trousers and shiny black hats, are strolling about, the rifles projecting from beneath their capes. Otherwise, nothing but the surrounding mountains and the winding road are in sight. Piling into the bus, for passengers seem to have appeared from nowhere, we present a merry picture. All are jovial, but the soldiers expostulate vociferously about being jammed like *sardinas en lata* (sardines in a tin). But the ride is worth the price. Mile after mile the road winds forth and back along the hillsides, gradually descending into a mountain-locked valley carpeted with a covering of luxuriant vegetation. Suddenly a village pops into view and for a second the panorama lingers. It is only for an instant, yet the impression remains. Every wall whitewashed and every roof of red tile, and all around, the green hills. Soon we are rattling along the narrow streets. Is this Old Spain? Not at all. However, a team of oxen hitched to a two-wheeled cart approaching with a load of great blocks of building stone lends color to the picture.

Again we are on our way as the train cuts its tortuous path through the mountains and ravines of Asturias. We have occupied first-class compartments and rarely has anyone brushed aside the curtain of our section to disturb the solitude of our reflections. We have tried the less comfortable second-class coaches, which had also accumulated a greater amount of the dust of the road. Here occasionally is found a business man, or perhaps as often an ecclesiastic. Ah, I think, an opportunity to strike up a conversation. The young clerical is all attention in an instant and for some moments we talk of commonplace affairs. Then he queries, *Ingleses? No, Americanos,* I reply. *De Nueva York?* he continues. No, *de California. Por Dios,* that is a long way off, isn't it? And he turns to his companions, but as the discussion proceeds with machine gun rapidity, the content thereof can only be inferred. Again we at times venture into the third-class coaches, though dirtier and even more uncomfortable than might be imagined. Here indeed we find the Spaniard just as he is. Hundreds of them, there seems to be no limit to the number of spitting, smoking humanity. Is there any need to relate that the latter has been termed the national vice? As the train trails on from station to station, there is a continual renewal of our traveling companions. Soon a grizzled old veteran with a bulging and noisy sack joins our group. The sounds emanating from his cargo seem to indicate a dozen fowl or more. Another sack-covered shape gives evidence of being nothing other than a swine, while all about us, above and below, are sacks and bags of more inanimate produce. Good company indeed, but who has seen the Spaniard without seeing him as he lives and travels?

Of travel he is indeed extremely fond. To have ridden *en los ferro-carriles* is to have made one's mark in life. Never does the train come sputtering and steaming into the town with no one to greet its arrival. It would rather seem that the population has turned out en masse to greet an old friend. Nor is the faithful train unmindful of these caressing touches. If it be a small junction he lingers listlessly on, ten, twenty, or even thirty minutes. The impatient traveler will spend many remorseful moments in Spain if he is in a hurry. But he will perhaps at the same time study with interest those who are now walking contentedly forth and back, smoking cigarettes, eating oranges and continually resisting the importunities of the ever present beggars. Eventually the station master will ring the little bell by the station door, but no one appears to mind him. After an interval of some minutes it clangs a second time. Perhaps the cautious soul will now climb back into the deserted coach but the master of the station must perform his duty a third time ere the train bids his friends farewell and hastens on to the next village at the rate of at least a dozen miles per hour. Now and then, it is true, a fast train is found on one or two of the main lines. But these are burdened with high fares and appear to exist for the benefit of the hurrying foreigner who has never learned the meaning of the word *mañana*. Truly no one but an Andalusian, even in Spain, fully realizes the significance of the term.

Andalusia is Spain's California. It is the land of the olive, the vine and the orange. Gay and temperamental, the inhabitants of this southland seem to have nothing in common with the people of the north. It is this region that played such an important part in the expansion of Spain into the New World immediately after its discovery. Seville became the capital of Spain's oversea possessions. Here were established the offices of colonial administration. The Casa Lonja, a huge two-story building constructed in 1598, served for a century as the seat of the House of Trade, a board which had complete control of American commerce. Today it stands as a memorial to the Spain that was. Within its walls are now stored thousands of bundles of documents relating to the Indies, for thus Spain referred to her colonies in North and South America. To this sanctuary come all students seeking to make a truthful narrative of the Spanish beginnings of our own south and west and of the lands to the south thereof. Seville in the colonial period was also the commercial center of Spain. At that time the mother country permitted only one port to carry on trade with her offspring, in order to enforce that monopolistic system which prevailed throughout Europe, of confining colonial trade to the mother land.

Andalusia has a strong Moorish tinge today. The Andalusian dialect with its soft expression is delightful to the ear. The Castilian, true enough, looks down upon his southern neighbor as he does upon everyone else. It was, par excellence, the region from which came the adventurers who left their old homes to found new ones and to acquire wealth in a New World. Accordingly it is not surprising that they, rather than the Castilians, gave to Spanish America the Andalusian accent.

To this region we come, and of its fame we have been fully informed. No matter where one may go in Spain, all will speak of Seville with the greatest enthusiasm, love and longing. It is the Paris of Spain, the home of joyful, happy and carefree Andalusians. We shall then not expect to find it a place of great political unrest. These Andalusians love their king, and he loves them. If Catalonia ever succeeds in breaking away and overthrowing the kingship, royalty will without doubt flee to Andalusia, a new kingdom will be set up and Seville will be its capital. I shall never forget the scene we witnessed in Seville on King Alfonso's birthday. The archives were closed, as was the case whenever the slightest excuse could be entertained. Taking an early *paseo*, my wife and I crossed the plaza of San Fernando, and beheld a large crowd. This plaza is the center of the city, and if anything happens it will undoubtedly occur there. On one side is the *ayuntamiento* or town hall, a building which dates from the time of Charles V. To see such a multitude of Andalusians assembled, and at nine in the morning, was truly remarkable for a winter day. It never happens unless some day of *fiesta* is at hand. Crossing the plaza, we paraded from one end of the town hall to the other. Soldiers and police constituted perhaps a third of those gathered. But we were not to see a street fight; not even a soap-box orator was visible. The mass shuffled a bit occasionally but all seemed to be peering in the same direction. Unable to understand this phenomenon, I saluted a policeman and requested, *Que hay?* (*What's up.*) He merely shrugged his shoulders and moved to one side. Thinking that he might have misunderstood, I appealed to one of his brothers-in-arms, and received the same noncommittal shrug. "Look, look, what is that up there?" My wife caught my arm and pointed to a balcony of the *ayuntamiento*. There stood two specimens of the finest of Spain's soldiery in full regalia. As steady as the rock of Gibraltar, these sentinels were guarding a life-sized painting of their beloved king. Nor did the number of watchers diminish during the day. 'Way into the night, group after group came to pay their respects to their monarch.

Concerning Andalusia much has been written. Anyone visiting Spain will inevitably go there, for to miss it is to forego a genuine treat. Every Spaniard expects to go there some time in his life. It is his ideal of happiness and joy. Moreover it is probably the most Spanish part of Spain. Here the women cling more tenaciously to the customs and dress of those who have gone before them. Their *fiestas* carry out the spirit of Andalusia, with its intense local color and feeling. At such times the women still wear their gorgeous shawls and mantillas; while in places other than Andalusia gowns modeled on Parisian styles are becoming popular. Foreign influence is indeed increasing. English and Americans have become so numerous that social intercourse is almost entirely limited to one's own people. The number of tourists has steadily increased. The attitude of the typical Andalusian, in fact of every Spaniard toward the foreigner, has been characterized by an English observer: "The average Spaniard pictures the average Englishman as an aggressive person with prominent teeth, long whiskers, a sun helmet, a green umbrella and pockets full of gold." That the tourist has on the whole given the Spaniard slight opportunity to form different impressions is equally certain.

On his arrival in Seville the foreigner sees little to stimulate his admiration. The narrow and dirty cobblestone streets in southern Spain are the originals from which the usual representations of old Spain are taken. Having at length found reasonable accommodations the tourist spends a busy first day sightseeing and being seen, the latter particularly applicable if the tourist be a woman. Whatever anyone may do or say, the Andalusian gentleman considers it his birthright to gaze upon femininity long and ardently, nor does he hesitate to give oral expression to his feelings. That those from abroad fail to understand the Spaniard can thus be easily appreciated. In fact, the inhabitants of the Iberian peninsula have almost nothing in common with the Frenchman or the Englishman. A Briton in Paris could quite readily pass for a Parisian, while in Spain he would be classed as a complete *extranjero*, a foreigner. On the second day the newcomer's antipathy is greatly heightened, for then he will be ill and perhaps confined to his bed a day or two. The procedure is almost invariable.

Since it is the month of December, the stone walls and brick floors radiate an icy chill. I do not speak of the few foreign-priced hotels but of the Spanish dwellings, and these have no provision for modifying the harsh atmosphere. This is not strictly true, for shortly a *brasero*, the curious relic of a bygone age which will perhaps never leave Andalusia, may be introduced into the room. It is a wash-basin-shaped pan of approximately the same size, supported on three legs and standing about eighteen inches from the floor. In the *brasero* are placed a few coals, whereupon it is filled with charcoal. In the course of three or four hours the charcoal will be a glowing bed of live coals protected by a light covering of ashes and sending forth a slight ray of warmth. A *badila* (fire shovel) is applied occasionally for the purpose of brushing aside the ashes and exposing the coals. If one stands directly over the 'heater' or, better still, extends the rim of one's overcoat around it, a feeling of warmth may be temporarily experienced. But few save the Spaniard can bear the poisonous fumes given off by the charcoal. Indeed so fearful is he of contracting the much dreaded *pulmonía* that all windows and doors are closed tight. The action of the charcoal on the atmosphere can be imagined, and few venture into the Spanish home under such circumstances.

Before bidding Andalusia farewell, we must visit a cobbler. The cobblestones in the streets, which seem like so many little mountainous peaks, have robbed milady of a heel. Right around the corner we shall find the man we are seeking. Thither we proceed. But what has happened to the good man? Numerous times we have seen him in his little shop idling away the hours quarreling with his fellows about the merits of this or that bull-fighter. Today he seems surprisingly busy. Our *buenos* (good morning) is countered by a muffled *buenos*, but no one inquires our mission. At length when the cobbler feels that we have developed a proper appreciation of his importance, he will wait upon his customer. But beware. If milady must use the mutilated shoe Sunday morning, it is best to state that she must have it by Saturday at nine since she is taking the train at ten. Otherwise you will appear at four in the afternoon and doubtless find the shoe in the same condition as when entrusted to the cobbler's care.

This characteristic of delaying everything to a remote tomorrow is a familiar Spanish trait. Whatever your demand may be, the Spaniard replies with a cheerful *mañana*. It is by no means a recent development. In 1607 Sir Francis Bacon, in an official memorandum, referred to the notorious delays of the Spaniard and recorded the opinion of the Secretary of State, Lord Salisbury, that it was not due to "malice or alienation of mind from us," but in part to the multiplicity of Spanish tribunals, and in part to a psychological cause, to "the nature of the people and nation, which is proud and therefore dilatory, for all proud men are full of delays and must be waited on." Bacon added that Spain's continued delays had become a by-word throughout the world. "Wherein I think his Lordship might allude to the proverb of

Italy, *Mi venga la morte di Spagna,* Let my death come from Spain; for then it is sure to be long a-coming." Yet this was the time when Spain was at the height of her glory and achievement. So Havelock Ellis says: "Questions of national psychology are more complicated than we sometimes realize, and the incalculable men who make a country great may often display qualities unlike, and even the opposite of those which permanently mark the mass of their fellow-countrymen."

Bordering on the Mediterranean is the busy and populous east, a region closely watched today by those interested in Spain's development. It is different from any other part of Spain, a different ambition pervades the atmosphere. Men and women here are progressive, hard-working and well-informed. It is the storm center of Spain, at the same time holding the business intelligence and the best part of the country's energy. The spirit which animates them has indeed made little headway elsewhere in the peninsula. That spirit is one of revolution, of progress, and of self government. Barcelona with its large element of factory workers is the center of the affected area. Here propaganda from France, Italy and elsewhere readily filters in and finds fertile soil. For many years it has been a thorn in the side of the government, and recently pressure has been applied to the spur. They are not only intolerant of the ruling house and the Madrid government but they hate it. Republican government, with the Church deprived of its influence in the councils of the powerful, is their goal. During the three or four years following the war, this rancorous growth of republicanism intensified and broke out in spots hitherto less affected. The attack and murder of the archbishop of Saragossa in February appeared to indicate a growing spirit of disaffection. The government at the time was pledged to the separation of Church and State. The archbishop, knowing the strength of the clergy, announced that if this policy was adhered to, the Church would throw its influence against the government. The response was a shower of bullets from assassins. Thus agitation spread. The overthrow of the government recently was merely a verification of the import of the preceding events. The tottering monarchy, however, was able to retain sufficient props to bolster up its sway and to stay the hand of the revolutionist once more. How long the day can be staved off is a matter of doubt. At present all is very quiet. The broom of the new regime is sweeping terribly clean for a few days. However, if the past can give any clue to what will happen in the time to come, it will be for but a short while. The future alone can tell. Meanwhile it is not out of place to recall the opinion of the Spaniards themselves, that nothing good lasts long in Spain.